ERNST FRIEDRICH

War against War!

ERNST FRIEDRICH

War against War!

With a Foreword by
BRUCE KENT

SPOKESMAN
Nottingham

First published 1st May 1924
This facsimile edition published in 2014 for the
Bertrand Russell Peace Foundation by agreement.

Spokesman
Russell House
Bulwell Lane, Nottingham, NG6 0BT, England
Phone 0115 9708318
Fax 0115 9420433
e-mail elfeuro@compuserve.com
www.spokesmanbooks.com

ISBN 978 0 85124 831 8
A catalogue record for this publication is available from the
British Library
Printed in Nottingham by Russell Press Ltd (www.russellpress.com)

FOREWORD

War against War! is one of the most shocking books I have ever seen. As much a series of photographs as a book, it first appeared in 1924, the work of Ernst Friedrich, an anarchist, socialist, internationalist and peace worker.

Friedrich's aim was to make people understand what war actually means, and the horrors it inflicts on people and, indeed, on animals. Gruesome are the photos of maimed men with their faces blown half away. How did those wretched war victims get through the rest of their lives? Hidden in some home? We do not even know their nationalities: just human beings who went through the horrors of a war which should never have been fought.

Ernst Friedrich had avoided military service in the First World War, partly by being locked up because his radical ideas were thought to be evidence of insanity. Later, after playing an active part in post-war German politics, he began a peace museum in Berlin – which the Nazis ransacked, in 1933, and eventually turned into a torture chamber. Friedrich's peace views had made him notorious and, with the Hitler era, he fled to Belgium and then to France where, in both places, he began peace centres. His grandson, Tommy Spree, still runs the restored *Anti-Kriegs-Museum* in Berlin, and it is through his kindness that this edition appears.

There have been many editions of *War against War!* Each has captions to the pictures in four languages. The three permanent ones are English, German and French. In this edition the fourth language is Dutch, but there have been editions with Russian or Chinese instead.

The captions are sometimes even understated – for instance, on the photos of a military graveyard in France where, post war, all the German graves have been vandalised but the French ones honoured and covered in flowers. Hatred lives on long after war.

Astonishing, too, is the picture of the Russian military cemetery where each grave has its own cross. Private soldiers get very small ones. Officers very much higher ones. In those days, military rank evidently counted even in the next world. German dead, French dead, Russian dead, British dead – they are all here – half naked, limbs missing, lying in ditches, rotting together.

'The pride of the family' says one caption of a smart young soldier showing off his rifle. There he is on the next page, in half his uniform, dead and mutilated, being dragged away.

But this is not just a picture book. It begins and ends with a passionate plea to understand the causes of war and to take steps to prevent it, and is addressed 'To Human Beings in all lands!' Unite and work for world peace is Friedrich's plea, made especially to the mothers of the world.

Why has the Bertrand Russell Peace Foundation decided to bring out this new edition? Surely, it is because we are now being drenched with First World War centenary propaganda. 'It had to be fought.' 'The only way.' 'Poor little Belgium' (which had, by 1914, killed millions in the Congo.) No mention of Tsar Nicholas's passionate appeal for an end to the arms race. No mention of the women from many countries, who met in 1915 in The Hague, demanding a negotiated end to the slaughter. No mention of Pope Benedict XV's repeated calls for an end to it all.

Children are now, a hundred years later, heading for Flanders Fields at some public expense. Schools are busy promoting World War One enterprises. Military chaplains are on the road trying to show local communities how 'Faith' brings us all together at times of crisis. Baroness Warsi goes so far as to bring the Empire into play. Says she:

> 'Christians, Jews, Muslims, Sikhs and Hindus lying side by side, just as these men had fought side by side – proving that the fight for freedom truly transcended the boundaries of nationality and faith.' (*British Future* 2013)

Yet that colonial world was not one of liberty and democracy.

Was Friedrich's call for an end to war a waste of wind? Not at all; the United Nations Charter was eventually signed in 1945. According to the preamble to that Charter, the first aim of this new international institution was to do just what he wanted:

> 'To save succeeding generations from the scourge of war.'

We have made at least a little progress. With the Charter, countries gave up their individual right to decide on war. The United Nations is not a pacifist body and the right to immediate self-defence was left in place.

The major countries in western Europe will not go to war with each other again. There are some limitations on the sale of arms, without which most of the civil wars of today would be impossible. We do have, however defective it may yet be, an International Criminal Court. The UN Security Council has no right to authorise military action unless all non-violent ways of settling disputes have been exhausted. Conscientious objection is now a legally recognised human right, though this is not a right granted in many countries. The 16,000-plus UK conscientious objectors of the First World War did not suffer in vain.

But so many of the attitudes which Friedrich denounced are still there. Parts of the press can and do whip up nationalist fervour and persuade people to believe in grossly exaggerated threats. Bogus history continues to dominate. The arms sellers and 'defence' firms still have a baneful effect on public policy. Profit still counts, wherever it comes from. The weapons of today (e.g. landmines, depleted uranium shells) continue to kill long after wars are over.

With the energy and vision of Ernst Friedrich, we can move far further towards ending war than we have yet managed. To spend $1.7 trillion a year on war and weapons, as we do today, when billions live in abject poverty, is a scandal. I hope so much that this timely edition of *War against War!* will make many more people determined to bring that scandal to an end.

Bruce Kent
Movement for the Abolition of War
London
February 2014

ERNST FRIEDRICH

Krieg
dem
Kriege!

Guerre
à la
Guerre!

War
against
War!

Oorlog
aan den
Oorlog!

Verlag / Editeur / Published by / Uitgeber

1. INTERNATIONALES KRIEGSMUSEUM

BEGRÜNDET VON ERNST FRIEDRICH

BERLIN C 2 / PAROCHIALSTRASSE 29

Den Schlachtendenkern, den Schlachtenlenkern, den Kriegsbegeisterten aller Länder ist dies Buch freundlichst gewidmet.

★

Aux Etats-Majors, à tous les Patriotes dans tous les pays, ce livre est poliment dédié.

★

To those who plan battles — to those who lead battles — to war enthusiasts of all countries — this book is dedicated.

★

Minzaam opgedragen aan de ontwerpers en leiders der veldslagen, aan de oorlogsdweepers aller landen.

Wer will der erste sein?

Hier, in diese Rubrik können sich die Herrscher und Regierungen derjenigen Länder der Reihe nach eintragen, die die Wahrheit fürchten und darum dieses Buch verbieten.

Qui passera le premier?

Cette rubrique est réservée à l'inscription des noms des monarques, des gouvernements et des pays qui craignent la verité et pour cela défendent ce livre.

	Name Nom Name Naam	Staat Etat State Staat	Datum Date Date Datum	Bemerkungen Observations Remarks Opmerkingen
1.				
2.				
3				
4.				
5.				
6.				
7.				
8.				
9.				
10.				
11.				
12.				
13				

Who will be the first?

Here, in this rubric may register the rulers and governments of those countries who fear the truth and who forbid this book.

Wie wil de eerste zijn?

In deze rubriek kunnen de heerschers en de regeeringen zich na elkaar inschryven, die de waarheid vreezen en daarom dit boek verbieden.

Menschen aller Länder!

Ich, der ich „Deutscher" fälschlich werd' genannt statt einfach: Mensch. Ich rufe nach des Nordens kalter Zone und hin nach Afrika und nach Amerika, nach Asien und nach Europa.

All überall. wo Ohren sind zu hören, ruf' ich zwei Worte nur und dies sind:

Mensch und **Liebe.**

Und so, wie der Australier weint, wenn ihm ein Schmerz begegnet, und lacht und jubelt, wenn ihm Freude, Glück beschieden, so eben weinst auch du, mein Bruder Eskimo, so Afrikaner und Chinese, weinst auch du und du und du und ich.

So wie wir alle, alle Menschen Schmerz und Freude gleich empfinden, so lasset uns gemeinsam kämpfen gegen den gemeinsam grauenhaften Feind, den Krieg.

So wollen wir gemeinsam klagen, weinen über das verfluchte Massenmorden, an dem wir alle gleichen Teil der Schuld. So aber auch laßt freudig uns den Blick erheben ins Morgenrot des Friedens und der Freiheit:

In aller Vaterländer Vaterland, ins Vaterland der Menschen, und **dieses über alles!**

In vielen Büchern sind viel Worte für und gegen dieses teuflischste, gemeinste aller Staatsverbrechen aufgeschrieben.

Des bürgerlichen Dichters Kraft verherrlichte in Versen diesen „Krieg",

und der Prolet-Schriftsteller schrieb auflodernd g e g e n dieses Massenmorden.

Doch aller Wortschatz, aller Menschen, aller Länder, reicht in aller Gegenwart und Zukunft lange nicht, um dieses Menschenschlachten richtig auszumalen.

Hier aber ist das nüchtern-wahre, das gemein-naturgetreue Bild des Krieges — teils durch Zufall, teils durch Absicht — photographisch festgehalten.

Die Bilder dieses Buches von Seite 50 bis zum Schluß zeigen Aufnahmen, von der unerbittlich, unbestechlich photographischen Linse erfaßt,

vom Schützengraben und vom Massengrab,

von dem „Etappenleben", von dem „Feld der Ehre" und von anderen „Idyllen" aus der „Großen Zeit". Und nicht ein einziger Mensch in irgend einem Lande kann aufstehn und gegen diese Photos zeugen, daß sie unwahr sind und nicht der Wirklichkeit entsprächen.

Und kommt auch nicht und sagt:

„Wie schrecklich, daß man solche Bilder zeigt!"
Sagt lieber: „Endlich, endlich ist dieses „Feld der Ehre", ist diese Lüge von dem „Heldentod", vom „Vaterland", von „Tapferkeit" und allen anderen Phrasen,
ist allen diesem internationalen Schwindel die Maske endlich, e—n—d—l—i—c—h — abgerissen!!"

Dies Buch sei allen Kriegsgewinnlern, Schiebern und Kriegshetzern freundlichst zugeeignet,
und nicht zuletzt gewidmet auch den Königen, Generälen, den Präsidenten und Ministern a l l e r Länder.

Den Priestern aber, die die Waffen segneten im Namen Gottes, denen sei dies Buch als Kriegs-Bibel gewidmet!

Zeigt diese Bilder allen Menschen, die noch denken können!

Wer dann n o c h diesen Massenmord bejaht, den sperre man ins Irrenhaus,
den meide man, wie man der Pest ausweicht!

Es sei denn, daß die Nationalisten und Kriegshetzer, die Könige und Generäle u n t e r s i c h den Krieg zu führen wünschen,
auf e i g e n e Rechnung und Gefahr,
und keinen Menschen zwingen, gegen seinen freien Willen mitzumachen!

S o l c h einen Krieg wird jeder Pazifist und jeder Proletarier begrüßen!

D a n n r o t t e t e n s i c h e n d l i c h a l l e K r i e g s - b e g e i s t e r t e n f r e i w i l l i g g e g e n s e i t i g a u s , und dann wär Friede, ewiger Friede in der Welt!

Doch leider — sind die Helden für solch einen „Befreiungskrieg" (Befreiung von den Kriegshetzern und -schiebern) nicht zu haben.

Es fehlt an Mut den Schlachtendenkern, Schlachtenlenkern, s e l b e r in den Kampf zu ziehn
und s e l b s t den süßen „Heldentod" zu sterben.

Darum erfand man schöne Worte, wie: „Vaterland" und „Feld der Ehre",
sprach von „Verteidigung" und andern Lügen mehr.
Und wer sich nicht zum Tode ließ begeistern, durch Militärmusik und Lügenmärchen von dem „Feind", der „angegriffen",
den zwang man gegen seinen Willen in den Mörderkittel,
gab ihm Befehl zu morden und zu rauben für die Geldsack-Interessen.

Ich wüßte hier ein praktisch Beispiel, den Krieg in alle Ewigkeiten zu verhindern:
Vor vielen, vielen Jahren war der Arzt, so sagt man, fürs Leben seiner Patienten voll verantwortlich mit seinem e i g n e n Hab und Gut und Leben! —
Starb der Patient in Händen des Arztes, starb dieser selbst.
So wollte es Gesetz. —
Und so sei auch G e s e t z f ü r K ö n i g e, P r ä s i d e n - t e n, G e n e r ä l e und Z e i t u n g s s c h r e i b e r n i c h t z u l e t z t:

„Wer Menschen in den Krieg zwingt, oder aufhetzt zu dem Massenmorden, der sei verantwortlich mit seinem ganzen Hab und Gut und mit dem e i g n e n Leben für das Wohl und Wehe der Soldaten!

Der König, der zu seiner Fahne ruft, ergreife s e l b s t die Fahne!

So ein Soldat verarmt, so mag der König mit ihm betteln gehen!

Wenn Hütten niederbrennen in den Kriegen, so mögen auch die Schlösser und Paläste aufgehn in den Flammen!

Und immer, wenn ein Menschenleben zu beklagen an der Front, so mag ein König oder ein Minister a u c h auf dem „Feld der Ehre" ruhn für Vaterland!

Und je z e h n Zeitungsschreiber, die zum Kriege hetzen, setzt ein als Geisel für das Leben e i n e s Kriegers!"

Doch dies Gesetz wird kaum geschaffen werden,
und keine „Abrüstungs"- und „Friedens"konferenz wird meinen Antrag je beachten.
Drum laßt uns, die wir Kämpfer sind, im Kriege gegen Krieg,
laßt uns die Kriegsursachen und Zusammenhänge untersuchen, damit wir — ausgerüstet mit der Waffe der Erkenntnis und dem scharfen Schwert des Geistes — siegreich diesen Kampf bestehn!

Kriegsursache

Schon Plato, der geboren war 427 Jahre vor dem Nazarener, schon dieser Weise sagte seinerzeit:

„A l l e K r i e g e e n t s t e h e n n u r u m d e n B e s i t z v o n G e l d!"

Das ist so wahr gesprochen, wie selten wohl ein Wort!
Denn noch in allen Kriegen galt und gilt es:
Geld und Gut und Macht zu schützen oder zu erobern, und

Kriege wird's solange geben, solang das Kapital das Volk beherrscht und unterdrückt!

Wenn sich das internationale Kapital durch gegenseitige Konkurrenz bedroht fühlt,
und wenn die Schlotbarone und Fabrikbesitzer unter sich in Streit geraten,
dann rasseln sie mit Säbeln und mit Sporen, dann rufen sie:
„Das V a t e r l a n d ist in Gefahr!" (Gemeint ist mit dem Vaterlande stets der G e l d s a c k!)

Und sonderbar:
die Arbeitssklaven aller Länder lassen Pflug und Amboß stehen,
eilen zu den Waffen,
und schützen Gut und Leben ihrer Herren, mit ihrem eignen Blut und Leben.

Was sag ich? „S o n d e r b a r sei dies?"
Es ist natürlich! — Ist natürliche Unnatur!
Denn nicht nur Staatsmacht und Gewalt zwingt alle
„Untertanen", Thron und Geldsack stets zu schützen, und
dafür zu verrecken,
es hat in gleichem Maße und mit gleicher Kraft auch
g e i s t i g die Proleten unterjocht!
Das wird leicht übersehen,
und darum steckt noch so viel b ü r g e r l i c h e I d e o l o -
g i e im Proletariat.
Darum sag ich's immer wieder meinen Brüdern, den
Proleten, sag's den Klassenkämpfern:
M a c h t E u c h f r e i v o n b ü r g e r l i c h e m V o r -
u r t e i l !
K ä m p f t g e g e n d e n K a p i t a l i s m u s i n E u c h !
A u s E u r e m D e n k e n u n d a u s E u r e m T u n ,
s p r i c h t n o c h u n e n d l i c h v i e l v o n S p i e ß e r -
u n d S o l d a t e n t u m ,
u n d f a s t i n j e d e m s t e c k t n o c h s o e i n e i n -
g e d r i l l t e r U n t e r o f f i z i e r, d e r h e r r s c h e n
u n d b e f e h l e n w i l l, s e i ' s a u c h n u r ü b e r
e i g n e K a m e r a d e n, u n d ü b e r F r a u u n d
K i n d i n d e r F a m i l i e !"
Doch sag ich auch zu jenen bürgerlichen Pazifisten,
die nur mit Händestreicheln, mit Teegebäck und frommem
Augenaufschlag Kriege zu bekämpfen suchen:

„Kämpft gegen den Kapitalismus —
und Ihr kämpft gegen jeden Krieg!

D a s S c h l a c h t f e l d i n F a b r i k e n u n d i n
G r u b e n,
d e n H e l d e n t o d i n S i e c h e n h ä u s e r n,
d a s M a s s e n g r a b i n M i e t s k a s e r n e n,
k u r z u m: d e n K r i e g, d e n s c h e i n b a r e w i g e n
K r i e g d e r A u s g e b e u t e t e n g e g e n d i e A u s -
b e u t e r !

Seht — Ihr — das — alles — nicht?

Also heißt Krieg dem Kriege:
Krieg der Geschobenen gegen die Schieber!
Krieg der Betrogenen gegen die Betrüger!
Krieg der Bedrückten gegen die Bedrücker!
Krieg der Gepeinigten gegen die Peiniger!
Krieg der Hungernden gegen die Satten!

Kriegsverhinderung

Wohl ist das Kapital U r s a c h e jedes Krieges!
Doch S c h u l d am Kriege sind wir selbst!!
An uns Proleten liegt es, Krieg zu führen,
und ebenso liegt es an uns, die Kriege zu v e r h i n d e r n !
W e i g e r t   d e n   D i e n s t !
E r z i e h t   d i e   K i n d e r   s o ,   d a ß   s i e   s i c h
s p ä t e r   w e i g e r n ,   S o l d a t e n -   u n d   K r i e g s -
d i e n s t e   z u   t u n !
Wie viele übersehen allzuleicht, daß in dem eignen
H a u s e , in der F a m i l i e , der Krieg freiwillig vorbereitet
wird!!!
Und hier liegt aller Laster Anfang,
hier liegt der A n f a n g auch des K r i e g e s .
Die Mutter, die dem Kind auf ihrem Schoß, S o l -
d a t e n l i e d e r singt, bereitet Krieg vor!
Der Vater, der S o l d a t e n s p i e l z e u g seinem Kinde
schenkt, mobilisiert das Kindchen für den Kriegsgedanken!
Soldatenspielzeug ist der Judas, den Du Dir selbst ins
eigne Haus holst, ist Verrat am Menschenleben!
Bedenk dies eine stets:
Das kleine Helmchen von Papier gefertigt,
wird einst der Stahlhelm auf dem Kopf des Mörders!
Und hat das Kind erst mit dem Luftgewehr geübt, wie
selbstverständlich wird es später mit der Flinte schießen!
Das Säbelchen aus Holz geschnitzt,
wird einst das Schlachtenmesser, das sich bohrt in eines
Menschen Leib!
Ihr Eltern, die Ihr es nicht wollt,
daß Eure Söhne anderer Eltern liebevolle Söhne morden,

Ihr sollt bedenken, daß das Kind, das Ihr mit Helm, mit Säbel und Gewehr beschenkt, sich seine zarte Seele aus dem jungen Körper spielt!

Doch jene Kinder, die zur Liebe und zur Solidarität, zur unbedingten Achtung vor dem unverletzlich heilgen Menschenleben sind erzogen, die Kinder werden ganz bestimmt untauglich sein für Waffendienst und Kriegsverwendung.

Wir Kriegsdienstgegner müssen endlich allen Glorienschein und allen Hokuspokus, mitsamt dem glänzendbunten Flitterkram der Soldateska niederreißen, und das aussprechen, was dann noch übrig bleibt:

ein vom Staat bezahlter Berufsmörder,
der in staatlich konzessionierten Mörderschulen (genannt Kasernen) ausgebildet wird,
in Ausübung des schrecklichsten Verbrechens: des Menschen-Mordes!!!

Bringt das den Kindern bei!

Dann wird das Mädchen, von Natur bestimmt, das Leben fortzupflanzen und zu schützen, das Mädchen wird sich ekeln mit den Soldaten, seinen ganz natürlichen Feinden — den „Zuhältern des Todes" — rumzuflirten!

Dann wird der Knabe später nicht den Uniformrock tragen, weil er weiß: Es ist ein Mörderkittel!

So klar und deutlich müßt Ihr denken
und auch handeln,
wollt Ihr das Uebel an der Wurzel fassen!
Und sollte dennoch wieder Krieg ausbrechen,
dann konsequent und rücksichtslos:

Krieg dem Kriege!

Der Generalstreik sei die erste Waffe!
Die Männer werden Dienst verweigern!
Das wahre Heldentum liegt nicht im Morden,
sondern in der Weigerung, den Mord zu tun!
Füllt lieber alle Gefängnisse und Zuchthäuser,
und alle Irrenanstalten aller Länder,
als für das Kapital zu morden und zu sterben!

Noch ist der letzte schauerlichste Krieg nicht ausgebrochen, der Gas und Gift und Flammen speien wird, auf Menschen, Tiere, Häuser.

Es liegt in u n s e r e n Händen, unserer Kraft, dies Ungeheuerlichste zu verhüten, zu verhindern!

Das große und erhabne Beispiel konsequenter Kriegsdienstweigerer sei uns Vorbild.

Sie haben lieber noch den Tod erlitten für ihr konsequentes „Nein!", als daß sie s e l b s t zum Mörder wurden!

„I c h   w i l l   n i c h t !"

Stärker als Gewalt, als Säbel und Gewehr
    ist unser Geist, unser W i l l e !
Sprecht nach der Worte drei: „ich will nicht!"
Gebt I n h a l t diesen Worten und alle Kriege
    sind in Zukunft unausführbar.
Denn was will alles Kapital der ganzen Welt,
was wollen alle Könige und Präsidenten machen,
wenn alles Volk in allen Ländern aufsteht
    mit dem Ruf:

„W i r   w o l l e n   n i c h t !"

Und F r a u e n   I h r :
Wenn Eure Männer dann zu schwach sind, dann
    schafft Ihr's!
Zeigt, daß das Band der Liebe zu dem Gatten stärker ist,
    als der Armeebefehl!
Laßt Eure Männer nicht zur Front!
Schmückt nicht mit Blumen die Gewehre!
Hängt Euch den Männern an den Hals!
Laßt sie nicht los, auch wenn das Abfahrtszeichen gellt!
Reißt alle Schienen auf, stellt Euch vor die Lokomotive!

**Frauen, schafft Ihr's,
wenn Eure Männer zu schwach sind!**

Mütter aller Länder vereinigt Euch!

ERNST FRIEDRICH
Ende Juli 1924

Aux Peuples de toutes les Nations!

Moi, qu'à tort, on appelle „Allemand" au lieu d'Homme tout simplement. Aux zones glaciales et torrides, à Afrique et à l'Amérique, à l'Asie et à l'Europe: Enfin à tous les pays où l'on est capable d'écouter, je ne crie que ces mots:

Humanité! Amour!

N'est-ce pas toujours la même douleur, la même joie qui font battre le coeur de l'Australien, du Chinois, de l'Esquimau et de l'Africain?

Unis que nous sommes par ces sentiments naturels; réunissons-nous donc aussi contre cet ennemi terrible, commun à tous, l a   g u e r r e !

Pleignons et pleurons en commun les victimes de ce massacre maudit, dont la faute incombe à tous; mais levons aussi joyeusement nos regards à l'aurore de la paix et de la liberté, à la patrie des patries, à la patrie de l'homme: **Vive cette Patrie!**

Beaucoup de livres ont été écrits pour et contre la guerre; ce crime diabolique des Etats. Le génie du poète bourgeois l'a glorifiée en vers et en prose, et l'écrivain prolétaire en des paroles vengeresses en a décrit toutes les monstruosités.

Mais aucune parole d'homme d'un pays quelconque ne suffira pour tout l'avenir à peindre ce massacre d'hommes.

Voici donc dans ce livre, fixée à l'aide de la photographie, moitié par hasard moitié par intention, la véritable face de cette guerre naturaliste, désenchanteresse, révoltante.

Les images de ce livre, à partir de la page 50 jusqu'à la fin montrent des aspects (saisis par la lentille photographique, impitoyable et incorruptible) de la tranchée-abri et de la fosse commune, de la vie dans les étapes, du champ d'«honneur», et d'autres idylles du «grand temps».

13

Pas un seul homme dans aucun pays ne peut s'élever en témoin contre ces photographies en disant qu'elles ne sont pas vraies, ou bien qu'elles sont en contradiction avec la réalité.

Qu'on ne vienne pas non plus me dire; Quelle horreur que de montrer de telles gravures.

Qu'on me dise plutôt, quel bonheur, on a enfin démasqué les mensonges de ce «champ d'honneur», de cette »mort des braves«, de cette interprétation de mot «partrie», de toutes ces duperies internationales.

A tous les charlatans patriotes et instigateurs de guerre, ce livre est dédié.

Aux Rois, Empereurs, Présidents de Républiques, Ministres, Généraux; et surtout aux Prêtres, qui dans chaque pays bénissaient les armes et glorifiaient la guerre, au nom du Dieu juste, du Dieu bon.

Si, après avoir montré ces images vraies à tout homme capable de penser, il en reste un capable de consentir de nouveau à cet «Assassinat» en masse, qu'on l'enferme comme fou, qu'on le fuit comme on fuit la peste.

Si, les Rois les Généraux, les Nationalistes, désiraient faire la guerre e n t r e e u x, à leurs propres risques et périls, pourvou qu'aucun homme ne soit forcé d'y prendre part contre son gré, je dirais! T a n t m i e u x.

Une t e l l e guerre serait acclamée par tous les prolétaires, par toutes les victimes de la guerre. V o i l à u n b o n m o y e n d e s e «d é b a r a s s e r» à j a m a i s d e t o u s l e s t r a i n e u r s d e s a b r e s, q u i e n s'é g o r g e a n t e n t r e e u x v o l o n t a i r e m e n t, n o u s p e r m e t t r a i e n t e n f i n d'a v o i r l a p a i x «U n i v e r s e l l e».

Mais hélas! Je crains que ces «Rodomonts» ne fassent défaut pour une telle guerre de délivrance (délivrance des traineurs de sabre, et de patriotes). Les faux idéologistes et les meneurs de batailles manqueront de courage, pour marcher au combat, pour mourir de la belle «mort des braves».

Voilà pourquoi on a inventé les menteuses paroles de «Patrie», «Champ d'Honneur», «Alliance Défensive», et quiconque n'est pas heureux de mourir pour elles, par la musique militaire et les mensonges sur l'ennemi qui nous a attaqué, est quand même forcé de porter l'uniforme d'assassin, de tuer et de voler pour défendre les intérêts des escrocs.

Je connais un moyen pratique pour empêcher à jamais le retour des guerres: En des temps lointains, le médecin, dit on, était responsable de la vie de ses malades, tout son bien, même sa tête, en répondait: Si le malade mourait entre ses mains, le médecin lui-même devait mourir; telle était la loi.

Que l'on fasse donc une loi semblable pour les Empereurs, les Rois, les Présidents, les Ministres, les Généraux, et enfin pour les «journalistes»:

Quiconque force l'homme à la guerre, est responsable de la vie des soldats, ses biens propres, sa vie même en sont la garantie.

Le Roi qui appelle au drapeau, doit le porter lui-même. Un soldat mutilé, ruiné, le Roi accompagnera le mendiant.

Pour chaque chaumière incendiée par la guerre, le feu sera mis à un Palais.

Pour une vie d'homme perdue au champ d'honneur: Un Roi ou un Ministre devra mourir au champ d'«Honneur». Dix Journalistes seront pris comme otages pour répondre de la vie d'un seul soldat.

Malheureusement on ne fera probablements jamais cette bonne Loi; et aucune conférence Internationale en faveur de la Paix ne prendra comme base de discussion ma proposition.

En conséquence: Combattants que nous sommes dans la guerre contre la guerre, passons en revue les causes et les effets de la guerre, afin qu'armés du sabre tranchant du savoir, et de la force de la raison, nous puissions finir cette lutte en vainquer.

La cause des Guerres

Platon (né 427 ans avant le Nazaréen), ce sage de l'antiquité, a dit: « T o u t e g u e r r e a c o m m e o r i g i n e l e s r i v a l i t é s p o u r l a p o s s e s s i o n.»

Voilà une parole de vérité profonde; car toujours, dans toutes les guerres il s'agit de la protection ou de la conquête d'argent, de possession ou de pouvoir.

Donc tant que le Capital règne sur peuple et le maîtrise, il y a menace de guerre.

Le Capitalisme dans tous les pays se sentant menacé par la concurrence, les barons de l'usine, du rail et du commerce se quellerent, font entendre un bruit d'armes et crient:

SAUVEZ LA PATRIE (ce qui en réalité veut dire sauvez la c a i s s e).

Et, extraordinairement, les esclaves du travail dans tous les pays quittent charrues et enclumes et accourent défendre et protéger les biens et la vie de leurs tyrans, en risquant leur propre biens et leur propres vies.

Que dis-je! E x t r a o r d i n a i r e m e n t.

C'est naturel, c'est la nature dénaturée. Car ce n'est pas seulement la puissance directe de l'Etat qui force tous les sujets à protéger le trône et le sac d'argent et de périr pour eux, c'est aussi et surtout la puissance indirecte que ce même Etat exerce sur l'esprit du prolétaire. Voilà ce qu'on oublit de dire, pourqoui nous trouvons toujours tant d'idéologie bourgeoise dans le prolétariat.

Voilà pourqoui je ne cesse de dire à mes frères combattants prolétaires:

« D é l i v r e z - v o u s d e s p r é j u g é s b o u r g e o i s ; l u t t e z c o n t r e l e c a p i t a l i s m e d a n s v o s â m e s , v o s p e n s é e s e t v o s a c t i o n s s o n t e n c o r e e m p r e i n t e s d ' i d é e s d ' é p i c i e r s e t d e s o l d a t s , e t d a n s c h a c u n d e v o u s o n r e t r o u v e e n c o r e l e s o u s - o f f i c i e r , q u i v e u t c o m m a n d e r e t g o u v e r n e r a u m o i n s d a n s s a f a m i l l e ».

16

De même je dis à ces Pacifistes Bourgeois, qui ne veulent combattre la guerre qu'avec des caresses.

Combattez le Capitalisme et vous dompterez toutes les guerres.

Luttez contre le champ de bataille les fabriques et dans le mines; luttez contre la mort des braves dans les hôpitaux, dans les fosses communes des casernes (ces tristes maisons de ville).

En un mot faites la guerre des exploités contre les exploiteurs en résumé:

Guerre à la guerre cela veut dire:

Guerre des exploités contre les exploiteurs.

Guerre des trompés contre les trompeurs.

Guerre des oppressés contre les oppresseurs.

Guerre des maltraités contre les maltraiteurs.

Moyens d'empêcher les Guerres

Bien que le Capital soit la cause de toutes les guerres, ce sont surtout les prolétaires qui en portent la responsabilité.

C'est au moyen de nos bras de prolétaire que l'on fait les guerres, c'est donc à nous de les empêcher.

Refusez le service militaire!

Elevez vos enfants de telle sorte qu'ils le refusent eux-mêmes un jour! Que tant de gens oublient que c'est dans la famille même que la guerre est préparée, voilà l'origine de tout vice.

La mère, qui à l'enfant sur ses genoux, chante des chansons militaires prépare la guerre.

Le père qui donne à l'enfant des jouets militaires prépare lui aussi la guerre.

Les jouets miltaires sont le Judas que tu apportes toi-même à la maison; ils sont une trahison à la vie humaine.

Souviens-toi que le petit casque militaire confectionné de papier sera un jour le casque militaire sur la tête de l'assassin, et le même enfant accoutumé à tirer le sabre aimera un jour se servir de la baïonnette fusil.

Parents, vous qui ne voulez pas que vos fils tuent les fils aimés d'autres parents, rappelez-vous que votre enfant en jouant avec des casques militaires, avec des sabres et des fusils, commence à corrompre sa jeune âme.

D'abord l'enfant s'est amusé avec le fusil à air comprimé et le sabre de bois et naturellement l'idée lui viendra de voir se transformer un jour ces armes inoffensives en armes de meurtres, le fusil portera au loin la mort, et le sabre de bois devenu baionnette ou couteau de tranchée ira feuiller la vie dans le corps des hommes.

Par contre les enfants habitués à l'amour, à la solidarité, au respect absolu de la vie, ne seront jamais capable de se soumettre à la guerre. Nous autres (les contempteurs de la guerre) nous devons arracher à la soldatesque, son auréole de faux-brillants.

Des assassins professionnels payés par l'Etat,
exercés dans les écoles d'assassins fournies par l'Etat
(autrement dit les casernes),
au crime le plus terrible au meurtre des hommes,
voilà ce qu'il faut faire voir aux enfants.

Alors la jeune fille, destinée par la nature, à procréer, refusera de s'allier avec les soldats, ses ennemis naturels, souteneurs de la mort.

Le garçon refusera de porter l'uniforme militaire, sachant que c'est un uniforme d'assassin.

Il est nécessaire que vos pensées et vos actions soient imbues de ces idées si vous voulez déraciner le mal.

GUERRE à la GUERRE !

La première arme la grève générale !

Les hommes refuseront le service militaire !

Le véritable héroisme n'est pas dans le meurtre, mais dans le refus du meurtre !

Que l'on remplisse les prisons, les maisons de force et les hospices d'aliénés de tous les pays, plutôt que de tuer ou de mourir pour les intérêts du Capital.

La dernière guerre épouvantable, qui crachera gaz, poison, flammes sur les hommes, sur les animaux et sur les maisons, n'est pas encore éclatée.

Dans cette dernière guerre nous avons vu des hommes préférant se faire condamner à mort, plutôt que d'assassiner eux-mêmes leu semblable.

Il faut que cela serve d'exemple pour tous.

Prolétaire, tu as dans les mains les moyens d'empêcher ce fléau.

Dis: « Je ne veux pas » et cela ne sera pas.

Contre ta volonté exprimée avec force, que pourront tes maitres: RIEN!

ET VOUS LES FEMMES!

Si, le jour venu vos hommes sont trop faibles ou trop lâches, vous devrez montrer votre volonté!

Vous montrerez que le lien qui vous attache à votre époux, à vos enfants, est plus fort qu'un ordre de mobilisation.

Ne souffrez pas que vos maris partent pour le front.

N'ornez pas de fleurs leurs fusils.

Empêchez le train de partir.

Pendez-vous aux cous de vos maris, de vos enfants.

Ne les lâchez pas quoique le signal du départ soit donné.

Arrachez les rails: Mettez-vous devant la locomotive.

Femmes c'est votre devoir si vous voulez protéger votre foyer.

Mères de tous les pays, unissez vous!

To Human Beings in all lands!

I, who am falsely called "German" instead of just simply "man", I call out to the icy regions of the North, I call out to Africa and to America, to Asia and to Europe.

To all regions that have ears to hear I call out but two words and these are

Man and **Love**

And even as the Australian weeps when he encounters pain, and laughs and makes merry when joy and happiness are granted him, even so dost thou weep, my brother Eskimo, and so, O African and O Chinese, weepest thou too and so weep I.

And as we all, all human beings, equally feel joy and pain, let us fight unitedly against the common monstrous enemy, War.

We shall unite in protesting against, in weeping over the accursed mass murders for which we all bear equal guilt. But let us also raise our eyes cheerfully to the red dawn of freedom and peace.

To the Fatherland of all Fatherlands, to the Fatherland of human beings **which stands above all!**

In many books have many words been written for and against this most diabolical, this meanest and lowest of all crimes of the State.

The bourgeois poet in his strength glorified this War in verse

and the proletarian writer wrote in glowing wrath a g a i n s t this mass murder.

But all the treasury of words of all men of all lands suffices not, in the present and in the future, to paint correctly this butchery of human beings.

Here, however, in the present book, — partly by accident, partly intentionally — a picture of War, objectively true and faithful to nature, has been photographically recorded for all time.

The pictures in this book from page 50 to the end, show records obtained by the inexorable, incorruptible photographic lens,
of the trenches and the mass graves,
of "military lies", of the „field of honour",
and of other "idylls" of the "Great Epoch".

And not one single man of any country whatsoever can arise and bear witness against these photographs, that they are untrue and that they do not correspond to realities.

And no one comes and says:
"O how frightful that such pictures should be shown!"

But he says rather: "At last, at last the mask has been torn away from this "field of honour"",
from this lie of an "heroic death", and from all the other beautiful phrases,
from all this international swindle the mask has at last, yea, at last, been torn away!! "

This book is dedicated to all war profiteers and parasites, to all war provokers,
and is consecrated also to the "kings", generals, presidents and ministers of a l l lands.

To the priests, however, who blessed the weapons in the name of God, this book is dedicated as a War bible!

Show these pictures to all men who still can think!

He who then s t i l l believes in this mass butchery, let him be locked up in a mad-house,
let us avoid him as we do the plague!

It may then be that the nationalists and war-provokers, the kings and the generals, may wish to carry on war a m o n g t h e m s e l v e s,
on t h e i r o w n acount and at t h e i r o w n risk, and that they force no man to join them against his will!

S u c h a war would indeed be welcomed by every pacifist and every proletarian!

T h e n a l l t h e w a r e n t h u s i a s t s w o u l d a t
l a s t o f t h e i r o w n f r e e w i l l e x t e r m i n a t e
o n e a n o t h e r,

and then we should have peace, eternal
peace on this earth!

But unfortunately these heroes are not to be had for
such a "war of liberation" (liberation from the war pro-
moters and profiteers).
They lack the courage, these war-thinkers and war-
leaders, to go themselves into the battle, and
themselves to die a sweet "heroic death".

That is why they invented such beautiful phrases as
"Fatherland" and "Field of Honour", and spoke of "defence" and uttered other lies.
And he who did not permit himself to be enthused to
death by military music and by lying legends of the
"enemy" of "the invaded",
him they forced against his will into the murderer's
uniform,
him they ordered to murder and to rob for the interests
of the money-bags.

I know of one practical way of preventing war for all
time to come.

Many, many years ago the doctor, it is said, was fully
responsible with his own life and property for the life
of his patients.
If the patient died at the hands of his doctor, the latter
died too.
Such was the law.
And so let there be also a law for kings, presidents, generals and, last but not least,
newspaper writers:

**"Whoever forces men into war or provokes them to
mass murders, shall be responsible with all his property and possessions and with his own life for the
safety and the sufferings of the soldiers.
The king who rallies peoble to his standard shall
himself bear the standard.
And if a soldier should be reduced to beggary, the
king shall go out begging with him.
If huts are burnt down in wars, so also shall palaces
and castles be set in flames.**

> And always, for each human life that is sacrificed at
> the front, shall one king or one minister rest in peace
> on the "field of honour" for the Fatherland.
>
> And t e n newspaper writers that agitate for war,
> shall be detained as hostages for the life of e a c h
> s i n g l e warrior!"

Such a law, however, will never come into being, and no
"disarmament" or "peace" conference will give heed to
my proposal.

Therefore let us, who are fighters, join in the war against
war,

let us examine the causes and the nature of war, so that,
armed with the weapon of knowledge and the sharp
sword of the mind, we may emerge victorious from the
fight.

The Cause of war

Long ago, Plato who was born 427 years before the
Nazarene, Plato, that wise man, said: —

"A l l   w a r s   a r i s e   f o r   t h e   p o s s e s s i o n   o f
w e a l t h ".

That is as true a word as ever was spoken.

For to the present day in all wars the object is to protect
or to seize money and property and power; **and there
will always be wars so long as Capital rules and oppresses
the people.**

When international capital finds itself threatened by
mutual competition,

and when the furnace-barons and factory owners begin to
have differences, among themselves,

then they rattle their sabres and spurs and they call out:
"The C o u n t r y is in danger!" (They mean by "country"
always the m o n e y - b a g s !)

And wonderfully enough

the working slaves of all lands abandon their plough and
their anvil,

they hasten to arms,

and protect the life and property of their masters with
their own blood and life.

What did I say? "That this is s t r a n g e ?" No, it is quite natural — a natural monstrosity!

For it is not the state power and force alone that compels all "subjects" to protect the throne and the money-bags, and to die for them.

Capital has not only e c o n o m i c power in its hands, it has, in equal measure and with equal power, subjected the proletariat also i n t e l l e c t u a l l y.

This fact is easily overlooked and there still remains, therefore, so much b o u r g e o i s i d e o l o g y in the proletariat!

I, therefore, always say to my brothers, the proletarians, I say to the class-war fighters: —

"F r e e   y o u r s e l v e s   f r o m   b o u r g e o i s   p r e-j u d i c e s !

F i g h t   a g a i n s t   c a p i t a l i s m   w i t h i n y o u r s e l v e s !

I n   y o u r   t h o u g h t s   a n d   i n   y o u r   a c t i o n s t h e r e   s t i l l   l u r k s u n s p e a k a b l y m u c h o f t h e p h i l i s t i n e   a n d   t h e   s o l d i e r, a n d   a l m o s t   i n   e v e r y o n e   t h e r e   i s   h i d d e n a   d r i l l e d   s u b a l t e r n, w h o   w i s h e s   o n l y   t o d o m i n a t e   a n d   c o m m a n d,   e v e n   i f   i t   b e o v e r   h i s   o w n c o m r a d e s   a n d   o v e r   h i s   w i f e a n d   c h i l d r e n   i n   h i s   f a m i l y !"

But I also say to those bourgeois pacifists, who seek to fight against war by mere hand caresses and tea-cakes and piously up-turned eyes: —

"F i g h t   a g a i n s t   C a p i t a l i s m   —   a n d   y o u f i g h t   a g a i n s t   e v e r y   w a r !

T h e   b a t t l e - f i e l d   i n   t h e   f a c t o r i e s   a n d t h e   m i n e s, t h e   h e r o's   d e a t h   i n   t h e   i n f i r m a r i e s,   t h e m a s s   g r a v e s   i n   t h e   b a r r a c k s, i n   s h o r t,   t h e   w a r, t h e   a p p a r e n t l y   e t e r n a l w a r,   o f   t h e   e x p l o i t e d   a g a i n s t   t h e   e x p l o i-t e r s !

Do — you — not — realise — all — this?

The war against war signifies: —

The war of the victimised against the profiteers!
The war of the deceived against the deceivers!
The war of the oppressed against the oppressors!
The war of the tortured against the torturers!
The war of the hungry against the well-fed!"

The Prevention of War

It is true that capital is the c a u s e of every war.

But the g u i l t of war rests on our shoulders.

It is we proletarians that make the conduct of war possible, it is for us likewise to p r e v e n t wars!

R e f u s e t o s e r v e !

B r i n g u p y o u r c h i l d r e n s o t h a t t h e y m a y l a t e r r e f u s e t o r e n d e r m i l i t a r y a n d w a r s e r v i c e !   ·

How very many ligthly overlook the fact that in one's own h o m e , in the f a m i l y , war is being spontaneously prepared!

And here lies the beginning of all evils, here lies the b e g i n n i n g also of w a r !

The mother that sings s o l d i e r s ' - s o n g s to the baby on her lap, prepares for war, yes, she prepares for war!

The father that makes gifts of t o y s o l d i e r s to his child mobilises the child for the war idea!

The toy soldier is the Judas that you yourself bring into the home, is the betrayal of human life! Remember always this one thing:

The little helmet made of paper will one day be a steel helmet on the head of a murderer!

And if the child has once practised with his air-gun, how natural it is that he should in later years shoot with a rifle!

The little sabre carved of wood

will some day become the battle-sword that pierces the body of a human being!

Ye parents that do not wish

that your sons should murder the dear sons of other

parents, you should remember that the child whom you present with a helmet and sabre and gun, plays his tender soul to death out of his young body.

Those children, however, who are educated in love and solidarity, and are brought up to respect unconditionally the inviolable sanctity of human life, these children will most certainly be u n f i t for arms and war-service.

We, opponents of military service, must finally destroy the halo and the humbug, and tear down the gaudy tinsel of the soldiery, and we must speak out what then still remains to be said:

a professional murderer paid by the state,

who is trained in murder-schools (caled barracks) privileged by the state.

in the carrying out of the most gruesome of crimes, the m u r d e r o f h u m a n b e i n g s!

T h a t is w h a t t h e c h i l d r e n s h o u l d b e t o l d !

Then indeed will the young girl, destined by nature to reproduce and protect life, be disgusted to flirt with the soldiers — her natural enemies — "t h e p i m p s o f d e a t h".

And the boy will later refuse to wear uniform because he knows: It is a m u r d e r e r ' s c l o a k !

It is with such clearness and precision that
you must think and also act,
if you wish to nip the evil in the bud!
And should war nevertheless break out,
then proceed consistently and unhesitatingly to

THE WAR AGAINST WAR!

Let the general strike be the first weapon!
The men will refuse service!
True heroism lies not in murder,
but in the r e f u s a l to commit murder.
Rather fill all prisons and workhouses
and all the mad-houses of all lands,
than murder and die in the service of Capital!

The last and most dreadful war has not yet broken out which will cast gas and poison and flames on human beings and animals and houses.

It lies in o u r hands, in our power, to prevent, to hinder, this most dreadful tragedy.

Let the great, inspiring example of consistent conscientious objectors be our model.

They suffered death for their consistent "No!" rather than themselves become murderers!

I WILL NOT!

Stronger than all violence, than the sabre and
    the rifle, is our spirit, is our w i l l !
Repeat these three words: "I will not!"
Give c o n t e n t to these words and all wars
    in future will be impossible.
What then will all Capital of the whole world,
what will al the kings and presidents do,
when the intire people in all lands arise with
    the cry:

WE WILL NOT!
AND YOU WOMEN!

If your husbands should be too weak, then carry
    out the work yourselves!!
Prove that the bond of love with the husband is
    stronger than an army order!
Do not let your men go to the front!
Do not decorate their rifles with flowers!
Cling to the necks of your husbands!
Do not let them go even when the order to depart calls!
Tear up all the rails, throw yourselves before the loco-
    motives!

WOMEN! REALISE THIS
IF YOUR HUSBANDS SHOULD BE TOO WEAK!

Mothers of all lands unite!

ERNST FRIEDRICH
End of July, 1924

Menschen van alle Landen!

Ik, die ten onrechte „Duitscher" genoemd word, in plaats van eenvoudig: M e n s c h , ik roep naar het koude Noorden, naar Afrika en Amerika, naar Azië en Europa

Overal heen, waar ooren zijn om te hooren, roep ik twee woorden, deze twee:

M e n s c h en L i e f d e.

Zooals de Australiër weent, als hem leed wedervaart, en lacht en jubelt, wanneer hem vreugde en geluk ten deel valt, zoo weent ook gij, mijn broeder Eskimo, gij Afrikaner, gij Chinees, zoo weent een ieder, gij en ik.

Zooals wij menschen alle op dezelfde wijze smart en vreugde ondervinden, zoo willen wij ook gemeenzaam strijden tegen den gemeenzamen, gruwelijken vijand, den oorlog.

Zoo willen wij gemeenzaam klagen en dezen massamoord vervloeken, waaraan een ieder van ons schuldig is. Maar vreugdevol willen wij den blik verheffen naar 't land van vrede en van vrijheid, waarvan het morgenrood ons tegenstraalt,

Naar 't vaderland van alle vaderlanden, naar 't vaderland der menschen en d i t b o v e n a l l e s.

In vele boeken zijn veel woorden voor en tegen deze duivelachtigste van alle staatsmisdaden geschreven.

De burgerlijke dichter verheerlijkte in verzen dezen „oorlog",
de dichter van het proletariaat schreef een felle aanklacht t e g e n dezen massamoord.

De woordenschat der menschen aller landen is echter niet in staat, in het heden of in de toekomst dit menschenslachten in zijn rauwe werkelijkheid te schilderen.

Hier echter is het natuurlijk-ware, het natuurgetrouwe beeld van den oorlog — ten deele door toeval, ten deele opzettelijk — photografisch vastgehouden.

De platen van dit boek, van pag ..... tot het einde zijn opnamen, door de onverbiddelijke, onomkoopbare photografische lens vastgehouden,

van loopgraven en van het massagraf, van het etappenleven, van het „veld der eer", en van andere „idyllen" uit den „grooten tijd".

En niet een mensch, in welk land dan ook, is in staat te zeggen, dat deze photo's nie aan de werkelijkheid beantwoorden.

En men zegge ook niet:

„Hoe verschrikkelijk zulke platen te toonen!"

Zegt liever: „Eindelijk, eindelijk, is dit „veld der eer", is de leugen van den „heldendood", van het „vaderland", van „dapperheid" en alle andere schoone phrases,

is aan dit internationaal bedrog het masker eindelijk, ein—de—lijk—afgerukt!!"

Opgedragen zij dit boek:

aan alle O. W.ers en oorlogsophitsers en niet in het minst aan „koningen" en generaals, aan presidenten en ministers van alle landen,

en aan de priesters, die de wapens zegenden in naam van God!

Toont deze platen aan alle menschen, die nog denken kunnen!

Wie dan n o g dezen massamoord verdedigt, dien sluite men op in het gekkenhuis, dien schuwe men als de pest!

Tenzij de nationalisten en oorlogsophitsers, de koningen en generaals onder elkaar wenschen oorlog te voeren, voor eigen rekening en eigen risico,

en niemand dwingen onvrijwillig mee te doen!

Z u l k een oorlog zal ieder pacifist en ieder arbeider toejuichen!

D a n r o e i d e n t e n m i n s t e a l l e o o r l o g s- e n t h o u s i a s t e n z i c h v r i j w i l l i g w e d e r z i j d s u i t,

en dan zou er vrede, eeuwige vrede op aarde zijn!

Jammer genoeg zijn de helden voor zulk een „be-
vrijdingsoorlog" (bevrijding van de oorlogsophitsers en van
de O. W.ers) niet te vinden.

Het ontbreekt den oorlogsutbroeders, den veldheeren aan
moed, z e l f ten strijde te trekken, z e l f den „zoeten
heldendood" te sterven.

    Daarom bedacht men mooie woorden, zooals „vader-
land" en „veld der eer".

sprak men van „verdediging" en vele andere leugens.

En wie nite in geestdrift voor den dood ontvlamde door
soldatenmuziek en sprookjes oder „den aanvallenden
vijand",

dien dwong men tegen zijn wil het moordenaarspak aan
te trekken,

die kreeg bevel to moorden en te rooven voor de belangen
van den geldzak.

    Ik wist een praktisch middel, den oorlog voor immer
onmogelijk te maken:

voor vele, vele jaren was de arts, zoo verteilt men, voor
het leven van zijn patiënten verantwoordelijk met heel
zijn have en goed!

Stierf de patient onder zijn handen, dan stierf de dokter
ook.

Zoo wilde het de wet. —

En zoo make men een w e t v o o r k o n i n g e n , p r e -
s i d e n t e n , g e n e r a a l s e n n i e t h e t m i n s t
v o o r k r a n t e n s c h r i j v e r s :

    **„Wie menschen tot den oorlog dwingt, of ophitst tot
den massamoord, dien stelle men verantwoordelijk
met have en goed, met eigen lijf, voor wel en wee van
de soldaten!**

    **De koning, die tot zijn vaandel roept, zij zelf de
vaandeldrager!**

    **Wanneer een soldaat verarmt, dan ga de koning met
hem bedelen!**

    **Wanneer de hutten in den oorlog worden neergebrand,
dan make men slot en paleis ook tot een prooi der
vlammen!**

    En voor het leven van één krijger die voor het vader-

land den dood ingaat, sterve ook een koning of minister op het veld van eer!
En voor het leven van één krijger neme men tien krantenschrijvers die tot den oorlog ophitsen, als gijzelaars!"

Maar deze wet zal nooit gemaakt worden en geen ontwapeningskongres of vredeskonferentie zal dit voorstel in overweging nemen.

Daarom laten wij, die oorlog aan den oorlog zweren, de oorzaken van den oorlog in zijn samenhang onderzoeken, opdat wij, toegerust met het zwaard des geestes, in dezen strijd de overwinnaars zijn.

De oorzaak van den oorlog

De wijze Plato, geboren 427 voor Christus, sprak reeds het woord:
„De oorzaak van den oorlog is gelegen in het bezit van geld!"

Weinige uitspraken zijn zoo juist als deze.

Want de verdediging of het „krijgen" van geld en goed en macht was steeds en is ook nu het doel van iederen krijg, en **zoolang zullen oorlogen bestaan, zoolang het kapitaal het volk beherrscht en onderdrukt!**

Wanneer gevaar dreigt voor het internationale kapitaal en ijzerkoningen, fabriekbezitters den strijd beginnen, dan hoort men sabel en sporengekletter, dan roepen ze: „Het vaderland is in gevaar!" (men zegt „het vaderland" en meent den geldzak).

En wonderlijk:
in alle landen velaten de slaven van den arbeid velden en fabrieken en grijpen naar de wapens om goed en leven van hun heeren te beschermen.

Wat zek ik? Wonderlijk is dit?

Het spreekt vanzelf! — Het is natuurlijke onnatuur! Want niet slechts staatsmacht en geweld dwingt alle „onderdanen" troon en brandkast tebeschermen, en daarvoor te krepeeren,

hat kapitaal heeft niet alleen de economische macht, maar ook op geestelijk gebied, heeft het de proletariers niet minder onderdrukt.

Dat wordt licht overzien
en daarom vindt men nog zooveel burgerlijke ideologie in
het proletariaat.

Daarom zeg ik steeds tot mijn broeders, den proletariers, zeg den klassenstrijders:
„Maakt u vrij van elk burgerlijk voor-
oordeel!
Strijdt tegen het kapitalisme in u!
Uw denken en doen bewijst hoeveel van
een burger, vaneen soldaatnoginuleeft,
in ieder bijna steekt nog iets van een
gedrilde onderofficier, die heerschen en
bevelen wil, al is het over eigen kameraden en vrouwen kind in de familie!"

Maar tot de burgerlijke pacifisten, die den oorlog met
zoete koek en vrome praatjes trachten te bestrijden, zeg ik:
"Bestrijdt het kapitalisme —
en gij bestrijdt den oorlog;
Het slagveld in fabrieken en in
mijnen,
Den heldendood in hospitalen,
Het massagraf in huurkarzernes,
Kortom den oorlog, den schijnbaar
eeuwigen oorlog, den uitgebuiten tegen
de uitbuiters!

Ziet — gij — dit — alles — niet?

Oorlog aan den oorlog, dat wil zeggen:
Oorlog der onderdrukten tegen de onderdrukkers!
Oorlog der bedrogenen tegen de bedriegers!
Orlog der gepijnigden tegen de pijnigers!
Oorlog der hongerigen tegen de verzagdigden!

De verhindering van den oorlog

Wel is waar is het kapitaal oorzaak van iederen
oorlog,
Maar schuldig aan den oorlog zijn wij zelf!

Het is aan ons, proletariërs, den oorlog te voeren, en aan ons is het den oorlog te v e r h i n d e r e n !

W e i g e r t   d i e n s t !

V o e d t   d e   k i n d e r e n   z o o   o p ,   d a t   z i j l a t e r w e i g e r e n   s o l d a t e n d i e n s t   e n   o o r l o g s w e r k t e   d o e n !

Hoevelen merken niet, dat zij vrijwillig in hun eigen h u i s , in hun f a m i l i e den oorlog voorbereiden!

H i e r is het, dat het kwaad begint, hier vind men ook de erste oorlogsoorzaak.

De moeder, die het kindje op haar schoot s o l d a t e n - l i e d j e s vorrzingt bereidt den oorlog voor!

De vader, die s o l d a t e n s p e e l g o e d aan zijn jongen geeft, wekt de oorlogsgedachte bij hem op!

Soldatenspeelgoed is de judas, dien gij uzelf in huis haalt,

is verraad aan menschelijk leven.

Bedenkt steeds dit:

de kleine helm van papier,

wordt eens tot staalhelm op het hoofd van den moordenaar!

En heeft het kind eens met het luchtgeweer gespeeld, dan zal het makkelijk later het geweer hanteeren! Het kleine sabeltje van hout wordt eens tot moordend staal!

Gij ouders, die niet wilt,

dat uw zonen de geliefde kinderen van andere ouders dooden,

gij moet bedenken, dat uw geschenk van helm en sabel en geweer, de teere kinderziel vergiftigt!

Maar d i e kinderen, opgevoed in liefde en solidariteit, in absolute achting voor het onaantastbaar menschelijk, leven, die kinderen zullen vast en zeker ongeschikt zijn voor wapendienst en oorlogswerk.

Wij, tegenstanders van den oorlog, moeten eindelijk allen oorlogsschijn en alle hokuspocus, met de geheele bonte schittering der soldateska ontmaskeren en wat er dan nog van overblijft, is dit:

een   door   den   staat   betaalde   beroepsmoorgenaar,

**die in door den staat geconcessioneerde moordenars-
scholen, (genaamd kazernes)**
geoefend wordt in de verschrikkelijkste misdaad: in men-
schenmoord!
L e e r t d a t d e n k i n d e r e n !

Dan zal het meisje, (van natuur bestemd het leven voort
te planten en te beschermen) een afschuw hebben met de
soldaten, haar natuurlijke vijanden, — d e s o u t e n e u r s
v a n d e n d o o d, — te flirten!

Dan zal de jongen niet de uniform meer dragen, omdat
hij weet:
het is een m o o r d e n a a r s p a k!

Zoo klaar en duidelijk moet gij denken en ook han-
delen,
wilt gij het kwaad in den wortel aantasten.
En mocht er toch een oorlog uitbreken,
dan consequent en zonder aarzelen:
Oorlog aan den oorlog!
De algemeene staking zij het eerste wapen!
De mannen moeten dienstweigeren!
Het ware heldendom ligt niet in moorden, maar in de
dienstweigering aan den moord!
Bevolkt liever alle gevangenissen en tuchthuizen,
En alle gekkenhuizen van de wereld,
Dan voor het kapitaal te moorden en te sterven!

Nog is de laatste verschrikkelijke oorlog niet uit-
gebroken, die gas en gift en vlammen spuwen zal op
mensch en dier en huis.

Wij hebben het in onze hand, wij hebben ook de
kracht dit vreeselijke te verhoeden, te verhinderen! Laten
wij het groote en verheven voorbeeld van de consequent
dienstweigeraars navolgen.
Zij kozen liever den dood voor hun consequent:
Neen!, dan dat zij zelf tot moordenaar werden!

"Ik wil niet!"

Sterker dan geweld, dan sabel en geweer, is onze
geest, is onze w i l!
Spreek deze woorden na, geeft i n h o u d aan deze
woorden: Ik — wil — niet!

Wat kunnen koningen en presidenten doen,
waneer het volk in alle landen opstaat met de roep:
En in toekomst zal geen oorlog mogelijk zijn.
Want wat wil al het kapitaal der wereld

"Wij willen niet!"

En gij vrouwen!

Wanneer uw mannen te zwak zijn speelt gij het klaar!
Bewijst dat uw liefde tot uw man sterker is dan een legerebevel.
Laat uw mannen niet naar het front gaan!
Tooit niet met bloemen de geweren!
Verhindert het vertrek der treinen!
Laat van uw mannen niet af, ook al weerklinkt het sein van vertrek!
Breekt de rails open, gaat voor de locomotieven staan!

Vrouwen, speelt gij het klaar, als uw mannen te zwak zijn!

Moeders van alle landen vereenigt u!

ERNST FRIEDRICH
Einde Juli 1924

Hoe de kinderen dor soldatenspeelgoed op den oorlog voor-
bereid worden!

How children are educated for war by means of toy soldiers!

Wie die Kinder durch Soldatenspielzeug für den Krieg vorbereitet werden!

Méthodes de préparer les enfants pour la guerre par les jouets
militaires!

Geef jullie kinderen niet dergelijk speelgoed.

Do not give the children such toys.

Gebt den Kindern nicht solche Spielsachen.

Ne donnez plus aux enfants de tels jouets.

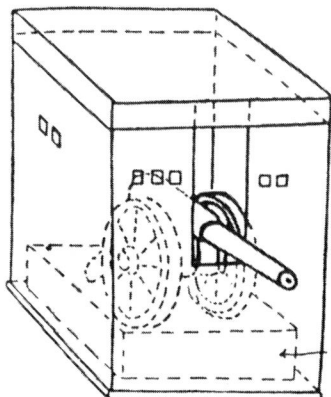

Holzstück, damit die Kanone bis zur Öffnung hinaufreicht.

Kanone aus Pappe und Holz.
Canon en carton et en bois.
Cannon of cardboard and wood.
Kanonnen van bordpapier en hout.

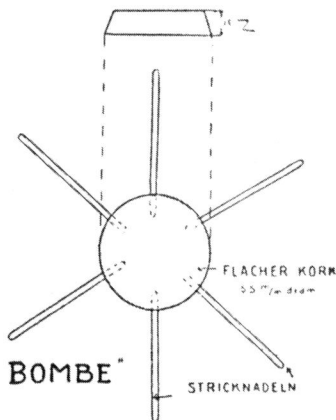

FLACHER KORK
0.5 "/m diam

BOMBE°

STRICKNADELN

Bombe aus Stricknadeln und Kork.
Bombe faite de bouchons et d'aiguilles à tricoter.
Bomb made of knitting needles and cork.
Bom van breinaalden en kurken.

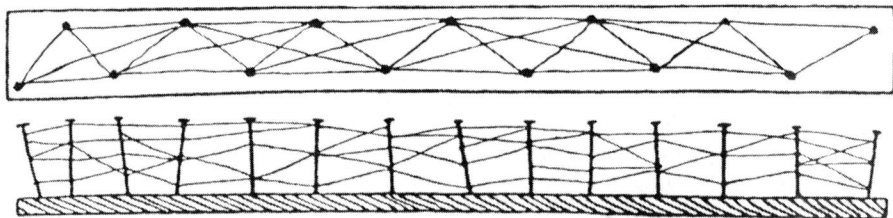

Stacheldraht aus Stecknadeln und Schnur (siehe Seite 103).
Treillis piquant confectionné d'épingles et de corde (à voir Page 103).
Barbed wire made of knitting needles and twine (to Page 103).
Prikkeldraad van spelden en snoer (zie blz. 103).

Formen zum Selbstgießen von Bleisoldaten.
Des moules à faire des soldats en plomb.
ulds to be used by the children themselves for making soldiers with molten lead.
Vormen om zelf soldaten van lood te gieten.

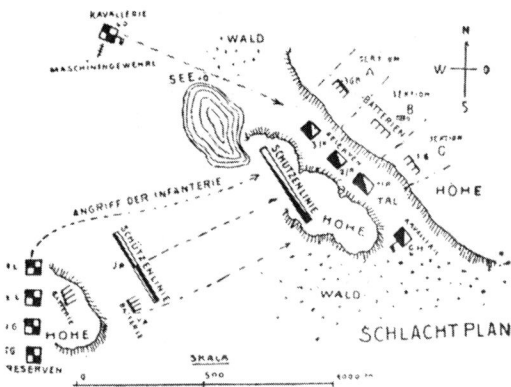

Ein „Schlacht"-plan.
Un ‚Projet de bataille'.
A „plan of battle".
Een „plan van een veldslag".

39

Papieren soldaten om uit te knippen en op te plakken.

Paper soldiers for cutting out an pasting.

Papiersoldaten zum Ausschneiden und Aufkleben.

Des soldats en papier à tailler et à coller.

De kerk als bondgenoot van het militairisme bij de opvoeding der kinderen voor het moordhandwerk. (De Kardinal van Westminster neemt tesamen met een generaal een parade af, uitgevoerd door de Engelsche padvinders.)

The Church as an ally of Militarism in the education of children for the profession of murder. (The Bishop of Westminster reviews, alongside of a General, a parade of English Boy Scouts.)

Die Kirche als Bundesgenosse des Militarismus bei der Erziehung der Kinder zum Mordhandwerk. (Der Kardinal von Westminster nimmt an der Seite eines Generals eine Parade englischer Jugendwehr ab.)

L'Eglise comme complice du militarisme chez l'éducation des enfants pour le métier de meurtre. (Le Cardinal de Westminster à côté d'un général examine les bataillons scolaires anglais.)

41

Di soort boeken kweekt bij de kinderen groote misdaden en wel het ver-
moorden van menschen!

Books of this kind educate the children to the greatest of all crimes: the
murder of human beings!

Bücher dieser Art erziehen die Kinder zum größten Verbrechen, zum
Menschenmord!

Des livres de cette espèce instruisent les enfants dans le plus grand
des crimes: le homicide!

Dit boek echter („Proletarischer Kindertuin") is bestemd, om de kinderen voor wederkeerigen steun en liefde aan te kweeken.

This book, however ("The Proletarian Kindergarten" is intented to educate children in mutual help and love.

Dieses Buch aber ist bestimmt, die Kinder zur gegenseitigen Hilfe und Liebe zu erziehen.

Ce livre-ci, au contraire, est destiné à instruire les enfants dans l'amour et le secours mutuel.

De moordenaar
The murderer
Le meurtrier
Der Mörder

De soldaat
The soldier
Le soldat
Der Soldat

Der Unterschied?
La différence?
The difference?
Het verschil?

Der kleine 13jährige Zeichner gab dazu folgende Erklärung:

„Der Unterschied zwischen Mörder und Soldat besteht darin, daß der Mörder ein Raubmörder, ein Lustmörder oder sonst ein Mörder ist. Dieser hat gegen das 5. Gebot gehandelt, also droht ihm der Tod oder das Gefängnis. Dagegen der Soldat ist auch ein Mörder — ein Berufsmörder — und zwar der größte, den es gibt — ein Massenmörder. Je mehr er mordet, je mehr Ruhm erwirbt er sich. Ihm setzt man den Lorbeer auf, ihm hängt man das Eiserne Kreuz und andere Orden um, wegen fingerfertigen Mordens. Er, der Soldat, ist der grausamste Mensch, den es gibt, so auf deutscher wie auf feindlicher Seite. Fluch denen, die sie das Morden lehrten und sie dazu veranlaßten. Also sind beide Mörder. Krieg bedeutet morden. Er bringt Hunger, Schmach, Elend, Not, Tod, Sorgen und Schmerzen.
Darum laßt ab von dem Morden und kehrt zum Frieden zurück."

Eine Kinderzeichnung und Text aus „Proletarischer Kindergarten".

Le petit dessinateur de treize ans donna l'explication suivante:

„La différence entre un meurtrier et un soldat consiste en ce que le meurtrier tue pour voler, pour contenter sa lubricité ou pour une raison quelconque celui-ci a péché contre le cinquième Commandement, donc la mort ou le prison le menacent. Le soldat, lui aussi, est un meurtrier — meurtrier de métier — et même le plus grand possible: un homicide en masse. — Mais il ose, lui, dédaigner le cinquième Commandement. Le meurtre lui est permis. Plus il tue, plus grande la gloire qu'il gagne On le couronne de laurier, on le décore de la 'Croix de Fer' et d'autres décorations à cause de son habilité dans l'art du meurtre. Le soldat est l'homme le plus cruel qu'on puisse imaginer, de même sur le côté des ennemis. Maudit ceux qui lui enseignent le meutre et le forcent à le commettre! Ils sont donc des meurtrier tous les deux. Car la guerre, cela veut dire: le meurtre. Elle nous amène la faim, la honte, la misère, la détresse, les soucis et les douleurs. Donc, ne touchez plus au meurtre et revenez à la paix.

Un dessin pris de 'L'Ecole enfantine prolétaire'.

The young 13 year old author of this drawing gave the following explanation of it:

„The difference between a murderer and a soldier consists in the fact that the murderer murders for plunder or for lust or fo ome other object. He acts against the 5th. commandment and is therefore threatened with death or imprisonment. The soldier, on the other hand is also a murderer — a professional murderer — and he is, in fact, the greatest of all murderers — a mass murderer. He may despise the 5th. commandment, he is permitted to murder. The more he murders, the greater is the fame he acquires. They crown him with laurels, they decorate him with the Iron Cross and other orders, in recognition of his dexterity in murdering. He, the soldier, is the cruellest being on earth, whether he be on the German side or that of the enemy. Cursed be those that have taught him to murder and caused him to murder! Both indeed are murderers. For war signifies murder. It brings in its traill hunger, disgrace, misery, suffering, death, anxiety and pain. So give up murdering and return to peace."

A child's drawing taken from „The Proletarian Kindergarten".

De kleine, 13jarige teekenaar gaf volgende verklaring daarbij:

„Het verschil tusschen moordenaar en soldaat bestaat daarin, dat de moordenaar een struikroover, een moordenaar uit wellust of de een of andere moordenaar is. Deze heeft tegen het vijfde gebod gehandeld, dus dreigt hem dood of gevangenis. De soldaat daarentegen is ook een moordenaar — een moordenaar van beroep — en wel de grootste, die er bestaat — een massale moordenaar. — Hij kon het 5. gebod verachten, hem was het moorden geoorloofd. Hoe meer hij vermoordt, deste meer roem hij verdient. Hij krijgt er zelfs een lauierkrans voor en als hij een heel handige moordenaar is, hangt men hem nog het Ijzere Kruis en andere ordeteekens om. Hij, de soldaat is de wreedstemensch, die er bestaat en wel op Duitsche zijde als bij de vijanden. Vloek over hen, die in het moorden onderwezen en hun aanleiding daartoe gaven. Dus alle twee zijn moordenaars. Want oorlog beteekent moorden. Hij brengt honger, hoon, ellende, nood, dood, zorgen en smart. Ziet dus af van het moorden en keert tot den vrede terug."

Een kinderteekening uit den „Proletarischen Kindertuin".

Wir haben keinen lieben Vater im Himmel.

Wär' einer droben in Wolkenhöh'n
Und würde das Schauspiel mitansehn,
Wie mitleidlos, wie teuflisch wild
Tier gegen Tier und Menschenbild
Wütet mit Zahn, mit Gift und Stahl,
Mit ausgesonnener Folterqual,
Sein Vaterherz würde es nicht ertragen,
Mit Donnerkeilen würde er dreinschlagen,
Mit tausend heiligen Donnerwettern
Würd' er die Henkersknechte zerschmettern!

Illustration und Text aus „Proletarischer Kindergarten"

Nous n'avons pas de Bon Père dans le ciel.

S 'il y avait quelqu'un dans les cieux,
Observant ce spectacle odieux
Comme, sans pitié et sans compassion, —
Victimes de leurs féroces passions —
Bête contre bête et bête contre homme,
Homme contre bête et homme contre homme,
Par les dents, e poison et le fer,
Ils se tuent mutuellement sous des tortures d'enfer
Son coeur de père ne pourrait le supporter,
Par des coups de foudre il devrait les frapper!
Par mille saintes tonnerres
Il écraserait les questionnaires.

Illustration et texte pris de 'L'Ecole enfantine prolétaire'.

We have no loving father in heaven.

If there were a Father in the heavens up above,
Who watched the dismal happenings here below,
Who witnessed the ruthlessness and the devilish fury
Of animals devouring animals and the children of man,
And man waging war on animals and on his own kind;
How they tear up one another with their teeth and
        with poison and with steel,
With deliberate and premeditated torture, —
His Divine Heart would endure it not
And He would hurl His thunderbolts into their midst,
And with a thousand lightnings
Would He destroy the muderers and executioners.

Illustration and text from „The Proletarian Kindergarten".

Wij hebben geen vader in den hemel.

Als er iemand boven in den wolken zou zijn,
Die dit schouwspel zou gadeslaan,
Hoe meedoogenloos, hoe duivelsch wreed
Dier tegen dier en mensch,
Mensch tegen dier en mensch
Tiert met de tanden, met gif en staal,
Met sluw verzonnen marteling,
Zijn vaderhart zou het niet dulden,
Met donder en bliksem zou hij er tusschen komen
Met duizend heilige donderslagen
Zou hij de beulen verpletteren.

Illustratie en tekst uit „Proletarische Kindertuin".

First the game, then the real hell.

EERST HET SPEL,
DAN DE HEL....

Erst das Spiel, dann die Hölle.

D'abord le jeu, puis l'enfer.

Kleine oorzaken — groote gevolgen.

Little causes — great consequences.

Kleine Ursachen — große Folgen.

Petit causes — grandes effets.

Uit de Augustusdagen 1914 — Geestdriftig . . . waarvoor? . . .

From the August days of 1914 — Enthusiastic . . . for what? . . .

Aus den Augusttagen 1914. — Begeistert . . . wofür? . . .

Des jours d'août en 1914 — Enthousiasmés . . . pour quoi? . . .

. . . voor het „veld van eer".

. . . for the "field of honour".

. . . für das „Feld der Ehre".

. . . pour le 'champ d'honneur'.

De eerste Duitsche reservisten gaan naat het front.

The first German reserves start for the front.

Die ersten deutschen Reservisten fahren zur Front.

Les premiers réservistes allemands partent pour le front.

De eerste technische successen.

The first technical successes.

Die ersten technischen Erfolge.

Les premiers succès techniques.

Vadertje als „held" in vijandelijk land
(Afbeelding voor het geïllustreerde familieblad).

Papa as "hero" in the enemy's country
(Picture for the illustrated Family Journal).

Vatting als „Held" in Feindesland
(Bild für das illustrierte Familienblatt).

Petit père comme 'héros' au pays ennemi
(Photographie pour le journal de famille).

Hoe men vadertje drie dagen latervond.
(Afbeelding, die niet in het „Familienblatt" werd gepubliceerd.)

How Papa was found two days later.
(Picture not published in the Family Journal.)

Wie man Vatting zwei Tage später fand.
(Bild, das im Familienblatt nicht veröffentlicht wurde;

Petit père — deux jours après.
(Aspect non publié dans le journal de famille).

Keizer Wilhelm II., bij de gratie Gods, komt van de bezichtiging van de slagvelden. (Op dat zijn koninklijke voet niet door den bloedgedrenkten grond besmeurd wordt is voor hem een extra loopplank gemaakt.)

William II, Kaiser by the grace of God, returns from an inspection of the battle-field. (In order to prevent his royal foot from being dirtied by contact with the blood-soaked land, a wooden foot-path was specially constructed.)

Kaiser Wilhelm II., von Gottes Gnaden, kommt von der Besichtigung des Schlachtfeldes. (Damit sein königlicher Fuß nicht vom blutgetränkten Boden beschmutzt wird, ist für ihn extra ein Holzsteg gebaut.)

Guillaume II., empéreur par la grâce de Dieu, revient de l'inspection du champ de bataille. (Pour que son pied royal ne soit pas sali par du sol ensanglanté, on lui a bâti exprès une passerelle de bois.)

„De oorlog is een element, van de door God bepaalde wereldorde."
(Graaf Moltke.)

"War is an element in the order ordained by God." (Count Moltke).

„Der Krieg ist ein Element der von Gott eingesetzten Ordnung."
(Graf Moltke.)

'La guerre est un élément de l'ordre émis par Dieu.' (Comte Moltke.)

De Hohenzoller verdeelt achter het front de eerste moordonderscheidingen.

The Hohenzoller distributes behind the front the first murder decorations.

Der Hohenzoller verteilt hinter der Front die ersten Mordabzeichen.

Le 'Hohenzoller' distribue derrière le front les premières décorations pour le meurtre.

Gezegde der Hohenzollerns: „. . . en nu zullen we ze eens dorschen, flink
erop losslaan!"

A saying of the Hohenzoller: ". . . and now let us thrash them!"

Ausspruch des Hohenzollern: „. . . und nun wollen wir sie dreschen!"

Parole du Hohenzollern: '. . . et maintenant: allons les rosser!'

In de etappe: de Duitsche kroonprins (met zijn hazewinden), die het gezegde uitvond: „I m m e r f e s t e d r u f f."

Behind the front; the German Crown Prince (with his greyhounds), who cultivated the expression "Keep hammering at it".

In der Etappe: der deutsche Kronprinz (mit seinen Windhunden), der den Satz prägte: „I m m e r f e s t e d r u f f".

A l'étape: le prince héritier de l'empire d'Allemagne (entouré de ses chiens de chasse), lequel a formé la phrase: 'En avant, sans façons!'

Aan het front: De Kroonprins is er niet bij.

At the front: the Crown Prince is not present.

An der Front: Der Kronprinz ist nicht dabei.

Au front: le prince héritier de l'empire d'Allemagne n'y est pas.

Flammenwerfer: Und wenn die Welt in Flammen steht . . .

Projectile de flammes: Bien que la terre soit en flammes . . .

Flammenwerper: En al staat de heele wereld in brand . . .

Liquid fire projectile: "And though the world should stand in flames . . .

De werking van de flammenwerpers:
       . . . en al zouden we ter helle gaan.

The effects of liquid fire:
       . . . and though it may perish in hell fire.

Die Wirkung des Flammenwerfers:
       . . . und wenn es in die Hölle geht.

Les effets du projectile de flammes:
       . . . bien qu'on marche à l'enfer.

Zij lachen en zijn blij . . .

They laugh and make merry . . .

Sie lachen und freuen sich . . .

Ils rient et se réjouissent . . .

. . . over de verminkte lichamen van hun „vijanden".

. . . over the mutilated bodies of their "enemies".

. . . über die zerfetzten Leiber ihrer „Feinde".

. . . sur les corps écharpés de leurs 'ennemis'.

Na het trommelvuur.

After the volley.

Nach dem Trommelfeuer.

Après le feu tambour.

Opruimingswerkzaamheden.

Clearing operations.

Opruimingswerkzaamheden.

Clearing operations.

Aufräumungsarbeiten.

Des travaux de débarassement.

Oorlogsmateriaal.

War material.

Kriegsmaterial.

Des matériaux de guerre.

Legerbericht: „Aan het front geen bijzondere gebeurtenissen."

Army report: "No particular occurrences at the front."

Heeresbericht: „An der Front keine besonderen Ereignisse."

Nouvelles de l'armée: 'Au front pas d'évènements notables.'

Legerbericht: „Aan het front is alles kalm."

Army report: "At the front all is quiet."

Heeresbericht: „An der Front ist alles ruhig."

Nouvelles de l'armée: 'Le front est tranquille'.

Menschelijke overblijfselen van een in elkaar geschoten pantserwagen.

Human remains of a battered armoured car.

Menschliche Ueberreste eines zusammengeschossenen Panzerwagens.

Débris de corps humains parmi une voiture cuirassée détruite.

An den Ueberresten eines heruntergeschossenen Fliegers.
A côte des débris d'un voleur qu'on a fait descendre par fusillade.
Bij de overblijfselen van een omlaag geschoten vlieger.
By the remains of an airman shot to earth.

Ein „berühmter" Fliegerheld, voller Stolz auf seine Beute.
Un héros de l'air fameux, gonflé d'orgueil de sa proix.
Een „beroemde" vliegenier, trotsch op zijn buit.
A "famous" air hero, full of pride over his booty.

Tooi Uw woning: Elk nummer een omlaag geschoten vlieger.

Decorate your home! Each number — an airman shot to earth.

Schmücke dein Heim: Jede Nummer — ein heruntergeschossener Flieger.

Bel décor de salon: Chaque numéro — un voleur détruit.

Courantenbericht: Het heeft Zijne Majesteit den Keizer behaagd om den beroemden vliegenier . . . naar aanleiding van zijn 7de overwinning in de lucht de ridderorde „Pour le mérite" (voor uitstekende buitengewone diensten) te verleenen.

Newspaper announcement: His Majesty the Kaiser has been graciously pleased to confer the order of "Pour le mérite" (for meritorious services) on our distinguished air hero . . . on the occasion of his seventh air victory.

Zeitungsnotiz: Seine Majestät der Kaiser geruhten, unserem berühmten Fliegerhelden . . . aus Anlaß seines 7. Luftsieges den Orden „Pour le mérite" (für hervorragende Verdienste) zu verleihen.

Note de gazette: Sa majesté, l'empereur, daigna donner à notre héros de l'air, à l'occasion de sa septième victoire dans l'air, la décoration 'Pour le mérite' (à cause de ses mérites extraordinaires).

Een „buitengewone" verdienstelijkheid.

A "meritorious" achievement.

Ein „hervorragendes" Verdienst.

Un mérite 'extraordinaire'.

De overblijfselen van een afgeschoten vlieger.

The remains of an airman shot to earth.

Die Ueberreste eines abgeschossenen Fliegers.

Les débris d'un voleur détruit à coups de fusil.

Keizer Wilhelm II: „Ik breng jullie herrlijke tijden te gemoet."

Kaiser William II.: — "I lead you towards glorious times".

Kaiser Wilhelm II.: „Ich führe Euch herrlichen Zeiten entgegen."

Empereur Guilleaume II.: 'Je vous conduis à des temps magnifiques!'

Deze plaats wordt vastgehouden . . .

The position will be held . . .

Die Stellung wird gehalten . . .

La position sera tenue . . .

. . . tot aan den laatsten man toe.

. . . to the last man.

. . . bis zum letzten Mann.

. . . jusqu'au dernier homme.

Het „veld van eer".

The "field of honour".

Das „Feld der Ehre".

Le 'champ d'honneur'.

Vergeten . . .

Forgotten . . .

Vergessen . . .

Oublié . . .

Kanonnevleesch . . .

Cannon fodder . . .

Kanonenfutter . . .

Mangeaille de canons . . .

Doodgeschoten zonen van het Schotsche Hoogland op de slagvelden van Frankrijk.

Sons of Scottish Highlanders lying dead on the battle-fields of France.

Erschossene Söhne der schottischen Hochwälder auf dem Schlachtfeld Frankreichs.

Les fils de la haute-futaie écossée, tués aux champs de bataille de la France.

Lijkverstarring: Fransche soldaat, die een kogel in het hart heeft gekregen, der-
halve de rechter hand stijf omhoog houdt.

Stiffening after death — rigor mortis. French soldier with heart-shot,
hence the right hand stiffly raised in the air.

Leichenstarre: Französischer Soldat mit Herzschuß, daher die rechte Hand steif
in die Luft erhoben.

Rigidité cadavérique Soldat français, blessé au coeur. Conséquence: la main droite,
élevée raide.

Russische soldat die door het hart geschoten is. (Door de terstond in-
getreden verstarring bleef deze soldaat gedurende den geheelen tijd van
het vuurgevecht in deze zelfde zittende houlding en werd door de vijandelijke kogels als 't ware doorgezeefd.)

Russian soldier shot through the heart. (In consequence of the stiffening
that immediately set in, the soldier remained in this sitting posture during
the wohle battle and was pierced through and through by enemy bullets.)

Russischer Soldat mit einem Herzschuß. (Infolge der sofort eingetretenen
Leichenstarre blieb der Soldat während der ganzen Dauer des Feuer-
gefechtes in dieser sitzenden Stellung und wurde von den feindlichen
Kugeln durchsiebt.)

Soldat russe avec un coup de feu au coeur. (En conséquence de la rigidité
cadavérique subite, le soldat restait dans cette position accroupie pendant
toute la fusillade et fut troué par les balles de l'ennemi.)

Duitsch haatgezang: Wat gaat ons Rus en Franschman aan . . .

German song of hate: What matters to us the Russian or the Frenchman . . .

Deutscher Haßgesang: Was schert uns Russe und Franzos . . .

Chanson de haine allemande: Nous nous fichons des Russes et des Français . . .

86

. . . Schot na schot en stoot na stoot.

. . . Shot against shot and blow for blow.

. . . Schuß wider Schuß und Stoß um Stoß!

. . . Coup contre coup et poussée contre poussée.

Voor de belangen van de kapitalisten . . .

For the interests of Capital . . .

Für die Interessen des Kapitals . . .

Pour les intérêts du capital . . .

. . . voor den roem der Monarchie,

. . . and the glory of the Monarchy.

. . . und den Ruhm der Monarchie.

. . . et pour la gloire de la monarchie.

... en hemelsche vrede lag in het bosch.

... and the peace of God lay upon the forest.

... und Gottes Frieden lag im Walde.

... et la paix de Dieu régnait dans la forêt.

Bajonetten steken omgekeerd in het zand, ten teeken, dat hier een zwaargewonde is blijven liggen.

Bayonets stuck in the sand, point upwards, showing that a heavily wounded soldier lies here.

Bajonette stecken verkehrt im Sand, zum Zeichen, daß hier ein Schwerverwundeter liegen geblieben ist.

Des baïonnettes, dressées de travers dans le sable, comme signe qu'à ce lieu un soldat gravement blessé a été abandonné.

„Slechts" een doode.

"Merely" a dead soldier.

„Nur" ein Toter.

Un mort "unique".

Moeders! Dat was het lot van jullie zoons in den oorlog: eerst vermoord, daarna geplunderd en eindelijk liet men ze liggen, als voedsel voor de dieren.

Mothers! That was the fate of your sons in the war: first murdered, then robbed to the skin and then left as grub for animals.

Mütter! Das war das Schicksal eurer Söhne im Krieg: Erst gemordet, dann bis auf die Haut geplündert und zuletzt liegengelassen, den Tieren zum Fraß.

Mères! Voilà le sort de vos fils dans la guerre: D'abord assassinés, puis pouillés jusque à la peau et enfin abandonnés comme mangeaille d'animaux.

De trots van de familie: (Een „interessante" kiek).

The pride of the family: (An "interesting" arranged photograph).

Der Stolz der Familie: (Eine „interessante", gestellte Photographie).

L'orgueil de la famille: (Une photographie "intéressante" posée).

De trots van de familie: (De keerzijde van de kiek, enkele weken later).

The pride of the family: (The other side of the picture, a few weeks later).

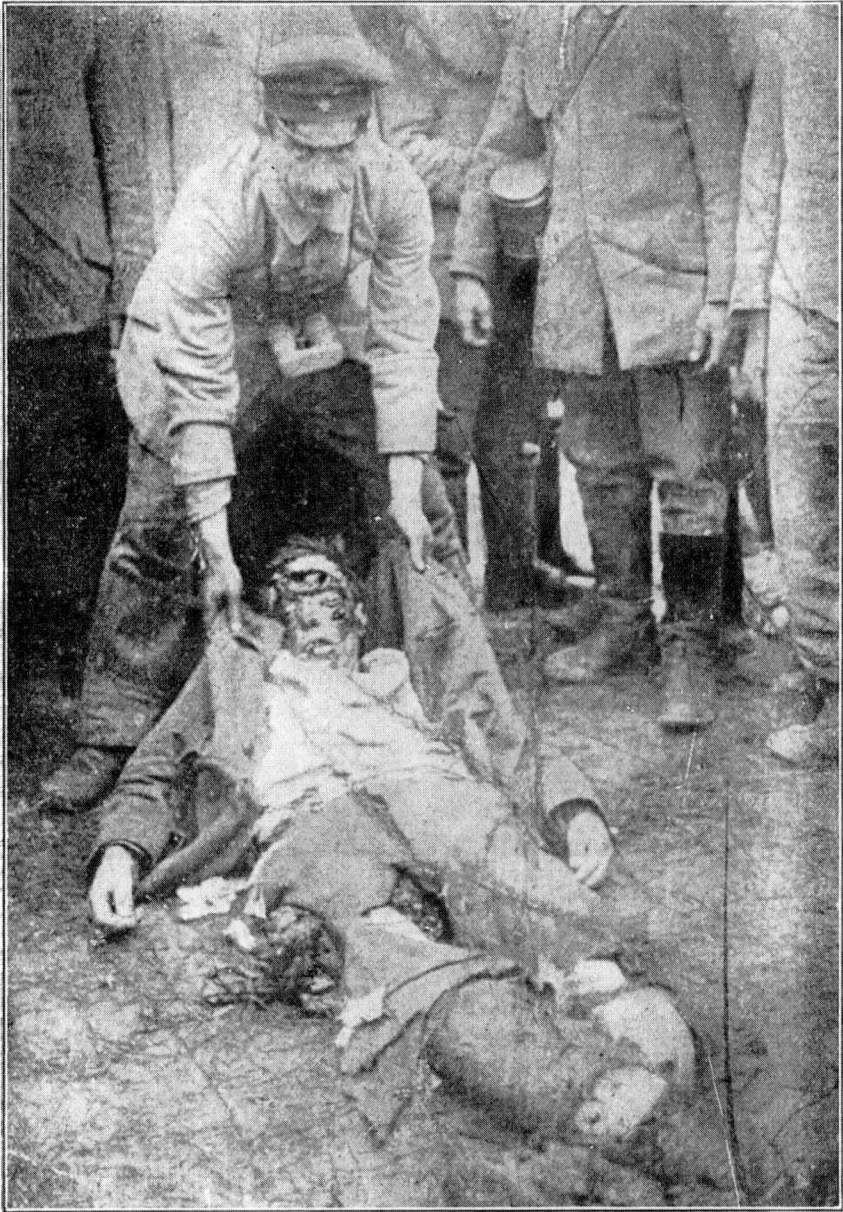

Der Stolz der Familie: (Die Kehrseite des Bildes, einige Wochen später).

L'orgueil de la famille: (Le revers de la médaille quelques semaines plus tard).

In den loopgraaf doodgeschoten.

Shot down in the trenches.

Im Laufgraben zusammengeschossen.

Tués dans la tranchée.

Het soldatenleven is verrukkelijk!

How magnificent is the soldier's life!

Herrlich ist das Soldatenleben!

Quelle joie que la vie de soldat!

Duitsch soldatenlied: Siegreich wollen wir Frankreich schlagen . . .

German soldier's song: In victory shall we vanquish France . . .

Deutsches Soldatenlied: Siegreich wollen wir Frankreich schlagen . . .

Chanson militaire allemande: Allons vaincre la France . . .

. . . sterven als een held.

. . . to die like a hero.

. . . sterben wie ein Held.

. . . mourir en héros.

Stuk geschoten haché-kanon.

Battered "stew cannon" (field kitchen).

Zerschossene Gulaschkanone.

Des marmites détruites.

„Helden te paard."

"Heroic horses".

„Pferdehelden."

'Des chevaux-héros.'

Paard in prikkeldraad.

Horse entangled in barbed wire.

Pferd im Stacheldraht.

Cheval dans l'abatis treillissé.

Moeders! . . . waarom hebt Ge d a t geduld ? ? ?

Mothers! . . . why have you tolerated t h a t ? ? ?

Mütter! . . . warum habt Ihr d a s geduldet???

Mères! . . . pourquoi avez-vous souffert cela???

Uitgeplunderd en laten liggen.

Plundered and abandoned.

Ausgeplündert und liegengelassen.

Déponillé et abandonné.

Terwyl voor het dorp Skoringi een parade plaats heeft, breekt er brand uit.
De parade mocht echter niet onderbroken worden en de manschappen niet
aan het blusschingswerk deelnemen, zoodat vrywel het geheele dorp af-
brandde.

While a parade was beeing held before the village of Skoringi, a fire broke
out. But the parade could not be interrupted nor the soldiers permitted to
hasten to put out the fire, so that almost the entire village was burnt down.

Während vor dem von den Deutschen besetzten Dorf Skoringi eine Parade
abgehalten wurde, brach Feuer aus. Die Parade durfte aber nicht unter-
brochen werden und die Mannschaften nicht zum Löschen eilen, so daß
nahezu das ganze Dorf niederbrannte.

Pendant une revue près du village Skoringi, le feu éclata au village. Comme
il fut défendu aux troupes d'interrompre la revue et d'aller faire jouer les
pompes, presque le village entier fut incendié.

Ik zal mijn menschen wel leeren sterven. (Pflanzer-Baltin, Oostenrijsche legeraanvoerder.)

Leave it to me to teach my men how to die. (Pflanzer-Baltin, Officer of the Austrian army.)

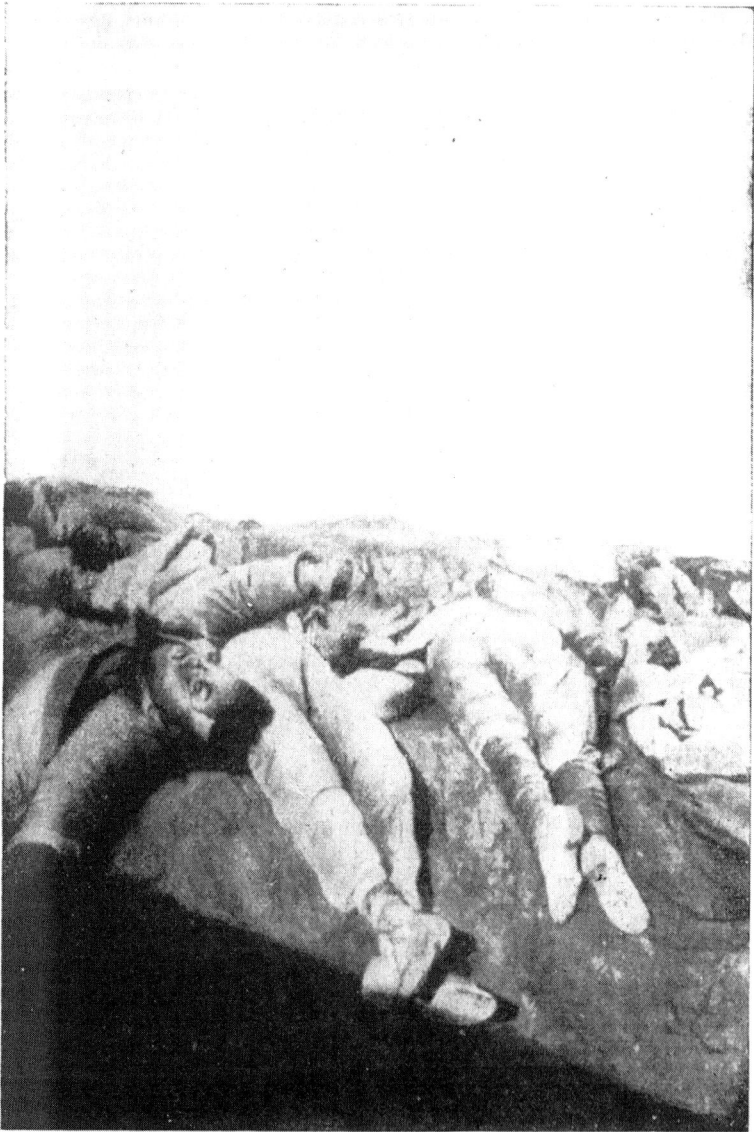

Ich werde schon meinen Leuten das Sterben lehren. (Pflanzer-Baltin, österreichischer Armeeführer.)

Je ne manquerai pas d'enseigner à mes soldats l'art de mourir. (Parole de Pflanzer-Baltin, général autrichien.)

„Kein schön'rer Tod ist in der Welt, als wer vorm Feind erschlagen . . ."
(Oud soldatenlied.)

"There is no sweeter death in the world than to die fighting the enemy . . ."
(Old soldiers' song.)

„Kein schön'rer Tod ist in der Welt, als wer vorm Feind erschlagen . . ."
(Altes Soldatenlied.)

'Il n'y a pas de mort plus belle que la mort du soldat tué en combattant
l'ennemi . . .' (Vieille chanson militaire.)

Geregeld bedrijf voor het gemeenschappelijke graf.

Regular work for the mass graves.

Regulärer Betrieb für das Massengrab.

Commerce régulier pour la fosse commune.

Gevangen Rus, dien men gedwongen heeft om zijn doode kameraden naar
volgorde „in te pakken". (Kiek is van bovenaf gezien, daar vandaan
de schuine stand van den Rus.)

Russian prisoner who has been forced to "pack" his dead comrades in a row.
(Picture seen from above, hence the inclined posture of the Russian.)

Gefangener Russe, den man gezwungen hat, seine toten Kameraden in Reih
und Glied zu „packen". (Bild von oben gesehen, daher die schräge Stellung
des Russen.)

Russe prisonnier, qu'on a forcé de ranger ses camarades morts. (Aspect
pris d'en haut. De cela résulte la position inclinée du Russe.)

De gevallen „helden" worden de helling af in het gemeenschappelijke graf gegooid (duidelijk ziet men de sporen van bloed en vuil bij de kalkvaten).

The fallen "heroes" are thrown down the slope into the mass grave (the blood and dirt-stains are clearly visible on the lime-tubs).

Die gefallenen „Helden" werden in das Massengrab den Abhang hinuntergeworfen (man sieht deutlich die Blut- und Schmutzspuren beim Kalkkübel).

On fait descendre les 'héros' morts du haut de la colline dans la 'fosse commune' (remarquez les restes de sang et de boue à côté de la caisse à chaux).

110

Hetzelfde gemeenschappelijke graf met een kijkje op de omlaaggegooide „helden". (Enkele van deze helden zijn van hun kleeren beroofd.)

The same mass grave showing a view of the "heroes" thrown in (some of these heroes have been robbed of their clothing).

Dasselbe Massengrab mit einem Blick auf die hinuntergeworfenen „Helden" (einige dieser Helden sind ihrer Kleider beraubt).

La même fosse commune faisant voir les 'héros' descendus (quelques-uns entre eux sont dépouillés de leurs habits).

De voorste lijken van dit gemeenschappelijke graf ghel van dichtbij gekiekt.

A close view of the foremost corpse in the mass grave.

Na hautnahme der vordersten Leichen dieses Massengrabes.

Aspect des corps de cette fosse commune pris de près.

Een Oostenrijksch „heldengraf".

An Austrian "hero's grave".

Ein österreichisches „Heldengrab".

Un 'tombeau de héros' autrichien.

Een ander „heldengraf": Boven het reds voltooide kruis
met hed stereotiepe opschrift: „voor het vaderland gevallen."

Another "hero's grave". Above, the already prepared cross
with the inscription: "Fallen for the Fatherland".

Ein anderes „Heldengrab": Oben das bereits fertige Kreuz
mit der stereotypen Aufschrift: „Fürs Vaterland gefallen".

Un autre 'tombeau de héros': Au dessus la croix déjà prête,
avec l'inscription stéréotype: 'Tombé pour la patrie'.

„Voor het vaderland" heeft men de gevallen helden op den voorgrond geheel uitgeplunderd.

"For the Fatherland" the fallen hero in the foreground was plundered to the skin.

„Fürs Vaterland" hat man den im Vordergrund gefallenen Helden völlig ausgeplündert.

C'est pour la patrie qu'on a complètement depouillé le 'héros' tombé au devant.

Aber das ganze „Heldentum" ist Lüge. Das Grauen ist Wirklichkeit.

Maar het heele „heldendom" is een en leugen. Het afgrijzen is werkelijkheid.

But all this "heroism" is a lie. Horror is the reality.

Le héroïsme, c'est le mensonge. Réalité, c'est l'horreur,

116

Opgezwollen en reeds in staat van ontbinding overgegane
lijken.

Bloated corpses in a state of put re faction.

Aufgequollene und bereits in Verwesung übergegangene Leichen.

Des cadavres gonflés et putriefiés.

In dem unter deutscher Verwaltung stehenden Gefangenenlager zu Bunzlau (Rumänien) wurden im Frühjahr 1917 für die an Cholera und Typhus
„verstorbenen" und v e r h u n g e r t e ñ (!) gefangenen Rumänen und Russen
jeden Monat zwei bis drei solcher Massengräber benötigt. In jedem solcher
Massengräber liegen 300 bis 500 Tote!

Duizende gevallen „helden" in het bosch.

Thousands of fallen „heroes" in the forest.

Tausende gefallener „Helden" im Wald.

Des milliers d' 'héros' tombés dans la forêt.

Text zum Bild auf Seite 118.

In het onder Duitsch bestuur staande gevangenenkamp in Bunzlau (Rumenië) waren in het voorjaar van 1917 voor de aan cholera en typhus „gestorven" en v e r h o n g e r d e! gevangen Rumenen en Russen maandelijks 2 tot 3 van dergelijke gemeenschappelijke graven noodig. In elk van deze gemeenschappelijke graven liggen 300 tot 500 dooden!

Text to picture on p. 118.

In the prisoners' camp in Bunzlau (Rumania) under German administration, 2 to 3 such mass graves were necessary every month for the Rumanian and Russian prisoners who in the spring of 1917 "died" of cholera and typhoid or were s t a r v e d t o d e a t h. In each such mass grave lie 300 to 500 corpses.

A l'image en page 118.

Dans le camp des prisonniers à Bunzlau (dans la Roumanie) sous l'administration allemande, en printemps 1917, on avait besoin par mois de deux à trois de ces fosses communes, contenants trois à cinq cents morts!

119

Hoe een generaal, die in de etappe gestorven is, begraven wordt . . .

How a general who passed away softly in slepp behind the front was buried . . .

Wie ein in der Etappe sanft entschlafener General beerdigt wurde . . .

De quelle manière on enterre un général, doucement expiré à l'étape . . .

120

. . . en hoe de aan het front geslachte proletariërs verstuwd werden.

. . . and how the proletarians massacred at the front were dispatched.

. . . und wie die an der Front abgeschlachteten Proletarier verladen wurden.

. . . et de quelle manière on expédiait les prolétaires, égorgés au front.

a) „Het veld van eer". De ernstige typhuszieken, die „toch" moesten sterven, kregen eenvoudig niets meer te eten, zoodat ze ellendig verhongerden Daarna gooide men ze in een gat in de aarde en zette er een kruis met het opschrift neer: „Voor het vaderland op het veld van eer gevallen."

a) The "field of honour". The serious typhoid patient who would die "in any case" was simply given nothing more to eat, so that he starved to death in utter misery. He was then thrown into a pit which was then filled in with earth. And a cross was set up on it with the inscription: "Fallen on the field of honour for the Fatherland".

a) „Das Feld der Ehre." Den schwer Typhuskranken, die „sowieso" sterben mußten, gab man einfach nichts mehr zu essen, so daß dieselben elend verhungerten. Dann warf man sie in ein Erdloch, scharrte sie zu und setzte ihnen ein Kreuz mit der Inschrift: „Fürs Vaterland auf dem Felde der Ehre gefallen."

a) Le 'champ d'honneur'. Aux soldats gravement malades du typhus, qui devaient mourir quand-même, on ne donnait tout simplement plus rien à manger, de sorte qu'ils mouraient de faim. Puis on les jetait dans une fosse, les interrait et leur érigeait une croix à l'inscription: 'Mort au champ d'honneur pour la partie.'

b) Uit de eigenaardige ligging van den verhongerden is duidelijk op te maken, dat de stervende met zijn laatste, wanhopige krachten geprobeerd heeft, om zich weer uit de kuil te redden. Hij is daarna echter ellendig omgekomen.

b) From the peculiar posture of the starved soldiers it may be clearly seen that the dying man attempted in his last desperate struggles to escape from the pit. But he died in suffering.

122

b) Aus der eigenartigen Lage des Verhungerten ist deutlich zu ersehen,
    daß der Sterbende in seinen letzten verzweifelten Kämpfen versuchte,
    sich wieder aus der Grube zu retten. Er ist aber dann elend verhungert.

b) L'attitude singulière du soldat mort de faim montre clairement que le
    mourant, dans ses dernières luttes désespérées, essayait en vain de se
    sauver de la fosse. Mais il est quand même péri de faim.

Volkeren van Europa, behoed uw heiligste goederen.

Peoples of Europe! preserve all that yon hold dear and sacred.

Völker Europas, wahrt eure heiligsten Güter.

Peuples de l'Europe gardez vos biens les plus précieux.

Het evenbeeld van God, met een gasmakser.
The „image of God" with a gas mask.

Das „Ebenbild Gottes" mit Gasmaske.
'L'image de Dieu' en masque protecteur contre le gaz.

125

Engelschen met gasmaskers.

Englishmen with gas maks.

Engländer mit Gasmasken.

Des Anglais, vêtus de masques protecteurs contre le gaz.

De eerste Engelsche gasmijn aan het Ijserkanaal 1914.

The first English gas mine on the Yser canal in 1914.

Die erste englische Gasmine am Yserkanal 1914.

La première mine à gaz au canal Iser en 1914.

Tevergeefsche herlevingspogingen aan een door gas vergiftigden.

Vain attempts to restore to life a gas victim.

Vergebliche Wiederbelebungsversuche an einem Gasvergifteten.

Des tentatives inutiles de revivication à un empoisonné de gaz.

„Na de veldslag": Den zwaargewonden heeft men natte doeken op
het hoofd gelegd, om ze tegen zonnebrand te beschermen.

After the "battle": To protect the heavily wounded against the
blazing sun, wet cloths were placed on their heads.

Nach der „Schlacht": Den schwer Verwundeten hat man zum
Schutz gegen den Sonnenbrand nasse Tücher auf den Kopf gelegt.

Après la 'bataille': On a mis sur les têtes des gravement blessés
des compresse mouillées contre le soleil brûlant.

Soldaten, die door het gas zijn vergiftigd en niet meer gered kunnen
worden, liggen stervend in de brandende zon.

Poison gas victims, who can no longer be saved, lie dying in the scorching
sun.

Gasvergiftete, die nicht mehr zu retten sind, liegen sterbend im Sonnenbrand.

Des soldats empoisonnés par le gaz, lesquels on ne peut plus sauver,
couchés mourants en plein soleil.

Eindelooze rij van gewonden.

Endless rows of heavily wounded.

Endlose Reihe von Schwerverwundeten.

Ligne infinie de gravement blessés.

Oostenrijksche soldaten bij hun „beulswerk" (Men lette op den soldaat, die den opgehangen man vasthoudt, om daardoor te kennen te geven, dat hij zelf de beul is en trotsch op zijn prestatie is.

Austrian soldiers at their "hangman's work". (Observe the soldier who touches the hanged man, in order to show that he himself is the hangman and is proud of it.)

Oesterreichische Soldaten bei der „Henkerarbeit". (Man beachte den Soldaten, der den Erhängten anfaßt, um damit anzudeuten, daß er selbst der Henker ist und auf seine Leistung stolz ist.)

Des soldats autrichiens au "travail de bourreau". (Prenez notice du soldat qui lui-même est le bourreau et qui touche le pendu pour faire voir qu'il s'en vente.)

Een kleine „soldatengrap". De beulen (Oostenrijksche soldaten) hebben al de opgehangen mannen „voor de grap" hoeden opgezet. De soldaat, die op de ladder staat, lacht grijnzend om zijn „grap" in het fotografisch toestel.

A small "soldiers' joke"! The hangmen (Austrian soldiers) have put hats on the heads of all the hanged men "by way of a joke". The soldier standing on the ladder grins in glee over his "joke" while being photographed.

Ein kleiner „Soldatenscherz". Die Henker (österreichische Soldaten) haben allen Aufgehangenen „spaßeshalber" Hüte aufgesetzt. Der auf der Leiter stehende Soldat grinst lachend über seinen „Scherz" in den photographischen Apparat.

Une petite 'plaisanterie de soldat'. Les bourreaux, des soldat autrichiens, pour 's'amuse', ont mis des chapeaux à tous les pendus. Le soldat sur l'échelle ricane de sa 'plaisanterie' en face de l'appareil photographique.

In het Oostenryksche leger werden gedurende den wereldoorlog vele
duizende menschen door den galg om het leven gebracht.

In the Austrian army during the World War, several thousand men were
executed by hanging from the gallows.

Bei der österreichischen Armee wurden im Weltkrieg viele tausend
Menschen durch den Galgen hingerichtet.

Pendant la guerre universelle, on exécuta dans l'armée autrichienne des
milliers d'hommes par la potence.

Slechts alleen by bet leger von aartsherzog Friedrich werden 11 400 galgen
op gesteld. (Volgens een andere statistiek: 36 000!)

In the army of the Grand Duke Friedrich allone, 11 400 gallows were erected.
(According to other statistics: 36 000!)

Allein bei der Armee des Erzherzogs Friedrich wurden 11 400 Galgen
errichtet. (Nach einer andern Statistik: 36 000!)

Dans l'armée du prince héritier Frédéric seulement on érigea 11 400
potences (d'après une autre statistique: 36 000!)

„Met sentimentaliteiten kan men geen oorlog voeren." (Hindenburg.)

"No war can be conducted by sentimentalities." (Hindenburg.)

„Mit Sentimentalitäten kann man keinen Krieg führen. Je unerbittlicher die Kriegsführung ist, um so menschlicher ist sie in Wirklichkeit." (Hindenburg.)

'Il n'est pas possible de pratiquer des sentimentalités dans la guerre.' (Hindenburg.)

De opgehangen priester als s c h i e t t e n f i g u u r !!! In de gevouwen
handen heeft men als teeken van den spot het kruis van den priester
gestoken. ——————— The hanged priest as a t a r g e t !!! In cynical irony,
a priest's cross was stuck into his bound hands.

Der aufgehangene Priester als S c h i e ß b u d e n f i g u r !!! In die gefes-
selten Hände hat man zum Zeichen des Spottes das Kreuz des Priesters
gesteckt. ——————— Le prêtre pendu, comme marionette!

137

Opgehangen vrouwen! (Op den voorgrond een Bulgaarsche soldaat, verder naar achteren de D u i t s c h e bondsbroederen.

Hanged women! (In the foreground a Bulgarian soldier, a little further behind, the G e r m a n allies.)

Aufgehangene Frauen! (Im Vordergrund ein bulgarischer Soldat, weiter hinten die d e u t s c h e n Bundesbrüder.)

Des femmes pendues. (Au devant un soldat bulgare, plus au fond les complices allemands.)

138

"But I say unto you: What ye have done to the meanest of my brothers, ye have done unto me."

„Ich aber sage Euch: Was Ihr getan habt einem unter diesen meinen geringsten Brüdern, das habt Ihr mir getan!" ———— "Mais moi, je vous dis: Ce que vous avez fait au moindre de mes frères, vous me l'avez fait à moi."

Oorlogsdienstweigeraars, die niet willen moorden, komen aan de galg.

Conscientious objectors, who did not wish to murder, — their
place was on the gallows.

Kriegsdienstverweigerer, die nicht morden wollen,
gehören an den Galgen.

Les refuseurs de la guerre, qui ne voulaient pas tuer — qu'on les pende!

140

Soldaten-„Handwerk" ist Mordhandwerk! (Die Berufsmörder stehen nach vollbrachter Arbeit stramm und lassen sich photographieren.)

Soldaten - werk is Moordshandwerk! (De beroepsmoordenaars staan na volbrachten arbeit rechtop en laten sich kieken.)

'The soldier's trade' is the murderer's trade! (The professional murderers, after having carried out their task, stand proudly to have themselves photographed.)

Le métier des soldats c'est le meutre; les assassins de métier, le travail fini, se font photographier.

141

Executie: a) „Ik heb hier slechts een ambt en geen meening." (Schiller.)

Shooting under martial law.
a) "I hold here only an office and no opinion." (Schiller.)

Standrechtliche Erschießung.
a) „Ich habe hier nur ein Amt und keine Meinung." (Schiller.)

Fusillade officielle. a) 'J'ai une fonction et pas d'opinion.' (Schiller.)

142

Executie. b) Maar God zeide tot Kain: Waar is je broeder Abel?

Shooting under martial law.
b) But God said to Cain: Where is thy brother Abel?

Standrechtliche Erschießung.
b) Aber es sprach Gott zu Kain: Wo ist Dein Bruder Abel?

Fusillade officielle. b) Mais Dieu demanda à Kaïn: Où est ton frère Abel?

Gezelschapsspel voor de officierstroep in Scharkow: Menschen, die men er van
verdenkt, dat ze bolsjewisten zijn, worden aan handen en voeten geboeid en . . .

Recreation for the officers' gang in Scharkow. Those "suspected" of bolshevist
tendencies are bound hand and foot and . . ,

Unterhaltungsspiel für die Offiziersmeute in Scharkow: bolschewistisch-„Ver-
dächtige" werden an Händen und Füßen gefesselt und . . .

Amusement pour les officiers à Scharkow: Des hommes, suspects au Bolchévisme,
sont liés aux mains et aux pieds et . . .

... neergeschoten.

... shot down.

... niedergeknallt.

... massacrés à fusil.

Andere Russische boeren, die om hun uiterlijk verdacht werden, dat
ze bolsjewisten waren en door de burgerlijke witte garde doodgeschoten
zijn.

Others, Russian peasants, who were shot down by the bourgeois white
guard, because their appearance led to the "suspicion" that they were
Bolsheviks.

Andere, von der bürgerlichen weißen Garde erschossene russische Bauern,
die wegen ihres Aussehens im „Verdacht" standen, Bolschewisten zu sein.

Des paysans russes, tués de la garde blanche bourgeoise à cause de leur
air bolchéviste.

146

Oorlogsstilleven.

Quiet life.

Kriegsstilleben.

Idylle de guerre.

„Dood door den strop!" Vier woorden als lood . . .

"Death on the gallows!" Four words heavy as lead . . .

„Tod durch den Strang!" Vier Worte wie Blei . . .

'Mort par la corde!' Parole lugubre et forte . . .

. . „Dood door den strop" — wat doet het er toe?
(Rudolf Herzog, een der meest gelezen Duitsche
romanschryvers. Kerstmis 1916.)

. . . "Death on the gallows" — what matters it indeed?
(Rudolf Herzog, one of the most widely read
German novelists Xmas 1916.)

. . . „Tod durch den Strang!" — was ist weiter dabei?
(Rudolf Herzog, einer der meistgelesenen deutschen Romanschriftsteller. Weihnachten 1916.)

. . . 'Mort par la corde — quatre mots — qu'importe!
(Rudolf Herzog, un des plus connus romanciers
allemands, à Noël 1916.)

Op weg naar het schavot.
Marching off to the gallows.
Départ pour le lieu d'exécution.
Abmarsch zur Richtstätte.

Voorlezen van het doodsoonis.
Reading out the sentence of death.
Lecture de la condamnation à mort.
Verlesung des Todesurteils.

Der Segen der Kirche.

„Unsere Schuld ist es nicht, wenn wir in der Blutarbeit des Krieges auch die des Henkers
verrichten müssen. Dem Soldaten ist das kalte Eisen in die Hand gegeben. Er soll es
führen ohne Scheu; er soll dem Feinde d a s B a j o n e t t z w i s c h e n d i e R i p p e n
r e n n e n ; er soll sein Gewehr auf ihre S c h ä d e l s c h m e t t e r n ; das ist seine heilige
Pflicht, d a s i s t s e i n G o t t e s d i e n s t." (Pfarrer Schettler.)

150

De zegen von de kerk.

„Onze schuld is het niet, wanneer wy in het bloedwerk von den oorlog ook nog beulswerk moeten verrichten. Den soldaat wordt het konde yzer in de hand gegeven. Hy moet het gebruiken zonder afschuw; hy moet den vijand de bajonet tusschen de ribben stooten; hy moet zyn geweer op hun schedel stukslaan; dat is zyn heilige plicht, dat is zyn godsdienst." (Dominee Schettler.)

The Blessing of the Church.

„It is not we that are to blame, if in carrying out the bloody tasks of the war, we are compelled to do also the duty of the hangman. The cold iron has been placed in the hands of the soldier. He is called upon to carry it without hesitation. He must run his bayonet into the ribs of the enemy. He must smash his rifle upon the enemy's skull. That is his holy duty, that is his divine service."

(Pastor Schettler.)

La bénédiction de l'Eglise.

"Ce n'est pas de notre faute, si dans le travail sanguinaire de la guerre, nous sommes forcés de faire aussi le travail du bourreau. On a remis le fer froid dans les mains du soldat. Il le doit manier sans aucun regret. Qu'il enfouce la baïonnette entre les côtes de l'ennemie! Qu'il lui casse le crâne à coups de crosse de fusil. Voilà son saint devoir, voilà son service divin!" (Schettler, curé.)

Armeniers, die uit hun vaderland zyn weggestuurd en onderweg door honger en uitputting zyn neergevallen. Op deze wyze zyn honderd duizenden ellendig verrekt. (Hoort het wel: honderdduizenden.)

Armenians who were dragged far away from their home and left on the road to die of hunger and exhaustion. (In this manner h u n d r e d s o f t h o u s a n d s died in untold misery and suffering.)

Armenier, die aus ihrer Heimat verschleppt wurden und unterwegs vor Hunger und Erschöpfung liegen geblieben sind. Auf diese Weise sind Hunderttausende elend verreckt. (Hört es wohl: Hunderttausende!)

Des Arméniens dérobés de leur patrie, qui sont restés en chemin épuises de faim et de fatigues. De cette manière des centaines de milliers devaient périr. (Ecoutez bien: des centaines de milliers!)

Verhongerd Armeensch kind: „Wij zijn tegenwoordig het hoogste volk!
Wij moeten het menschdom omhoog omhoog voeren en elk medelijden,
dat wij met laagstaande volkeren hebben es een zonde tegen onze taak.
(Paul Ernst den 22. 8. 1915 in de „Vossische Zeitung".)

Starved Armenian child: "We are today the greatest nation! We have
to lead humanity further, and every mercy shown to lower races is a crime
against our mission" (Paul Ernst on the 22nd of August 1915 in the
"Vossische Zeitung").

Verhungertes Armenierkind: „Wir sind heute das höchste Volk! Wir haben
die Menschheit weiterzuführen, und jede Schonung, die wir niedrigeren
Völkern angedeihen lassen, ist eine Sünde gegen unsere Aufgabe," (Paul
Ernst am 22. 8. 1915 in der „Vossischen Zeitung".)

Enfant arménien, mort de faim: Aujourd'hui nous sommes le peuple
supérieur à tous. Il est à nous de guider l'humanité, et tout ménage, que
nous montrons pour les peuples plus bas, est un péché contre notre vocation
(Paul Ernest dans la 'Voss. Ztg.', le 22 août 1915).

153

Verhongerde Armeensche kinderen.
Famished Armenian children.

Verhungerte Armenierkinder.
Des enfants armeniens morts de faim.

154

Succesvolle beschieting van Ostende.
Succesful bombardment of Ostend.

Erfolgreiche Beschießung von Ostende.
Bombardement de Ostende couronné de succés.

155

Duitsche troepen marcheeren op hun „zegevierenden" opmarsch door een
brandend dorp.

German troops in "victorious" advance march through a burning village.

Deutsche Truppen marschieren auf ihrem „siegreichen" Vormarsch durch ein
brennendes Dorf.

Des troupes allemands en leur marche 'victorieuse' passent un village
en feu.

156

... tot aan de laatste ademhaling van man en paard.

... to the last breath of man and horse.

... bis zum letzten Hauch von Mann und Roß.

... jusqu'au dernier soupir d'homme et de cheval.

Bekanntmachung!

Einwohner!

Wir führen nur Krieg gegen die feindliche Armee und nicht gegen die Einwohner. Trotzdem sind die deutschen Truppen häufig durch Personen angegriffen worden, die nicht zur Armee gehören. Man hat die **schoussliohsten Grausamkeiten** nicht nur an unseren Truppen, sondern auch an unseren Verwundeten und Aerzten verübt, die sich unter dem Schutz des Roten Kreuzes befinden.

Um diese Gewalttätigkeiten in Zukunft zu verhindern, befehle ich Folgendes:

1. Jede nicht militärische Person, die mit Waffen in der Hand angetroffen wird, wird ohne weiteres niedergeschossen; sie wird als ausserhalb des Völkerrechts stehend betrachtet.

2. Alle Waffen, Gewehre, Pistolen, Brownings. Säbel, Dolche usw. sowie **jeder** Explosivstoff sind durch den Ortsvorstand sofort dem deutschen Truppenbefehlshaber abzuliefern.

Wenn eine einzige Waffe irgendwo gefunden, oder irgend eine Feindseligkeit gegen unsere Truppen, Transporte, Telegraphen- und Eisenbahnlinien usw. begangen oder wenn dem Franktireurs Obdach gewährt wird, so werden die Schuldigen und die festgenommenen Geisseln ohne Pardon niedergeschossen. Ausserdem werden die Einwohner der betreffenden Ortschaft verjagt, die Ortschaften und Städte selbst werden zerstört und niedergebrannt. Wenn dergleichen auf einer Strasse oder in dem Gelände zwischen zwei Ortschaften vorkommt, so wird in derselben Weise gegen die Einwohner der beiden Ortschaften vorgegangen.

Ich erwarte, dass die Ortsvorstände wie auch die Bevölkerung durch geeignete Überwachung und besonnene Haltung über der Sicherheit unserer Truppen, wie auch über eigenen Sicherheit wacht.

Es geschieht dies nicht so treten die oben angekündigten Maßnahmen in Kraft.

Der Kommandierende General.

Proclamation!

Habitants!

Nous ne faisons pas la guerre contre les citoyens mais seulement contre l'armée ennemie. Malgré cela les troupes allemandes ont été attaqué en grand nombre par des personnes qui n'appartiennent pas à l'armée. On a commis des **actes de la plus lugubre cruauté** non seulement contre les combattants mais aussi contre nos blessés et nos médecins qui se trouvent sous l'abri de la croix rouge.

Pour empêcher ces brutalités à l'avenir j'ordonne ce qui suit:

1. Toute personne qui n'appartienne pas à l'armée et qui soit trouvée les armes entre les mains sera fusillée à l'instant; elle sera considérée hors du droit des gens.

2. Tous les armes, fusils, pistolets, brownings, sabres, poignards etc. et toute matière explosible doivent être délivrés par le maire de tout village ou ville aussitôt au commandant des troupes allemandes.

En cas qu'une seule arme soit trouvée dans n'importe quelle maison ou que quelqu'acte d'hostilité soit commis contre nos troupes, nos lignes télégraphiques, nos chemins de fer ou qu'on donne l'asile aux franctireurs, les coupables et les otages qui sont arrêtes dans chaque village seront fusilles sans pitié.

Or cela tous les habitants des villages etc. en question seront chassés, les villages et les villes mêmes seront démolis et brûlés. Si cela arrive sur la route de communication entre deux villages ou entre deux villages on agira de la même manière contre les habitants des deux villages.

J'attends que les maires ainsi que la population voudront assurer par leur prudente surveillance et combla la sûreté de nos troupes ainsi que la leur. Dans le cas contraire les mesures indiquees ci-dessus entreront en vigueur. — On ne donnera aucun pardon.

Le Général Commandant en Chef.

158

Proclamation!

Citizens!

We are carrying on war against the enemy army, not against the civil population. Notwithstanding this, the German troops have frequently been attacked by persons who do not belong to the army. The most detestable cruelties have been practised not only on our troops, but also on our wounded and our doctors who stand under the protection of the Red Cross. In order to prevent such acts of violence in future, I hereby issue the following order:

1. Every civilian found in possession of weapons shall be shot down without further notice and shall be regarded as standing outside international law.

2. All weapons, rifles, pistols, brownings, swords, daggers, etc. as well as all kinds of explosive material shall be handed up immediately through the mayor to the commander of the German troops. If a single weapon should be found anywhere or any act of hostility be committed against our troops, transports, telegraph and railway lines etc., or if franctireurs be given shelter, both the guilty persons as well as the hostages in custody shall be shot down without mercy. Besides, the inhabitants of the localities shall be driven out, the villages and towns themselves destroyed and burnt down. If similar acts be committed on a street between two villages, similar steps will be taken against the inhabitants of both the villages.

I expect that the local headmen as well as the population will, by appropriate supervision and a reasonable attitude, watch over the safety of our troops as well as their own.

Should this not be the case, the measures announced above will immediately come into operation.

The General in Command.

Proclamatie!

Inwoners!

Wij voeren alleen oorlog tegen het vijandelijk leger en niet tegen de inwoners. Desondanks zijn onze troepen veelal door lieden aangevallen, die niet tot het leger behooren. Men heeft niet alleen onze troepen maar ook onze gewonden en doktoren, die onder de bescherming van het roode kruis staan, de afschuwelijkste gruwelen doen wedervaren. Om deze daden van geweld in de toekomst te verhinderen, beveel ik het volgende:

1e. Iedere burger, die mit wapens in de hand aangetroffen wordt, wordt zonder pardon neergeschoten, hij wordt als buiten het volkerenrecht staand, beschouwd.

2e. Alle wapens, geweren, pistolen, brownings, sabels, dolken enz, alsmede ontplofbare stoffen moeten door den burgemeester onmiddelijk bij den Duitschen troepenbevelhebber ingeleverd worden. Zoo ergens ook maar een wapen wordt gewonden, dan wel de een of andere vijandelijke daad tegenover onze troepen, transporten, telegraafleidingen, spoorwegen enz, verricht wordt, of als aan franctireurs onderdak wordt verleend, dan worden de schuldigen en de in hechtenis genomen gijzelaars zoder pardon neergeschoten. Buitendien worden de inwoners uit de betrokken plaats verjaagd, de dorpen resp. steden zelf worden verwoest en platgebrand, Indien zulks op een weg tusschen twee gehuchten voorkomt, dan wordt op dezelfde wijze tegen de bewoners der beide plaatsen opgetreden.

Ik verwacht dat de burgemeesters als ook de bevolking door geschikte controle en een bedachtzame houding over de veiligheid van onze troepen, alsmede over hun eigen veiligheid zal waken!

Geschiedt dit niet, dan treden die boven aangekondigde maatregelen in werking.

De kommandeerende generaal.

BEKANNTMACHUNG

Am 29 September abends ist
nahe Löwen auf der Strecke
zwischen Lovenjoul-Vertryck die
Eisenbahn- und Telegrafenlinie
zerstört worden, anscheinend durch
Landseinwohner. Daraufhin sind
die beiden genannten dem Tatort
nächstgelegenen Ortschaften zur
Rechenschaft gezogen und Geiseln
festgenommen worden.

Um künftigen derartigen An-
schlägen wirksam vorzubeugen,
sind am 1.10.14. in allen grösseren
an der Eisenbahnstrecke deutsche
Grenze - Verviers - Lüttich - Löwen -
Brussel - französische Grenze bele-
genen Ortschaften GEISELN festgenommen worden.

Es wird der Bevölke-
rung bekannt gegeben,
dass diese Geiseln un-
nachsichtlich erschos-
sen werden, sobald der
geringste neue Zerstö-
rungsversuch an Eisenbahn,
Telegrafen oder Telephonlinien in der
Nähe der betreffen-
den Ortschaft gemacht
wird.

Löwen, [...] 1914.

AUF BEFEHL
[...]

Die Kommandantur

Proclamation

Pendant la soirée du 29 Septembre dernier, la voie du chemin
de fer et la ligne du télégraphe ont
été détruites entre Lovenjoul et
Vertryck, apparemment par les
habitants de la région. En conséquence, les villages environnants
ont été punis et ont dû livrer des
otages.

Pour éviter le renouvellement
de ces attentats, des otages ont
été constitués à partir du 1 Octobre 1914, dans toutes les localités
importantes situées le long de la
ligne frontière Allemande, Verviers-
Liège-Louvain - Bruxelles- frontière
Française.

Il est porté à la con-
naissance du public que
ces otages seront impi-
toyablement fusillés, si
la moindre tentative de
ce genre se renouvelle
contre les lignes du Chemin de Fer, du
Télégraphe ou du Téléphone, dans le
voisinage des localités
en question.

Louvain, le [...] 1914.

PAR ORDRE
[...]

La Commandanture

Bekendmaking

In den avond van 29 September
laatstleden, zijn het spoor van den
IJzerenweg en de Lijn van den
Telegraaf vernietigd geweest tusschen Lovenjoul en Vertryck, waar-
schijnlijk door inwoners dier streek.
Bijgevolg zijn de naburige dorpen
gestraft geworden en hebben moeten
gijzelaars leveren.

Om in het vervolg die aanslagen
te voorkomen, zijn er nieuwe gijzelaars gesteld geworden (te beginnen
van 1 October 1914) in alle belang-
rijke gemeenten gelegen langsheen
de lijn der Duitsche grens, Verviers-
Luik - Leuven - Brussel - Fransche
grens.

Er wordt ter kennis van
het publiek gebracht
dat die gijzelaars onver-
biddelijk zullen doodge-
schoten worden ingeval
de minste poging van
dien aard zich zou her-
nieuwen tegen de lijnen
van den IJzerenweg, van den Telegraaf of
van den Telefoon in de nabij-
heid dier gemeenten.

Leuven, den [...] 1914.

OP BEVEL
[...]

DE KOMMANDANTUR

Belgische gedeporteerden, die gedwongen werden om in de Duitsche
amunitiefabrieken te werken.

Deported Belgians compelled to work in German ammunition factories.

Belgische Deportierte, die gezwungen wurden, in deutschen Munitions-
fabriken zu arbeiten.

Des déportés belgiques, forcés de travailler dans les fabriques de munition
allemandes.

„Wie vor 1000 Jahren die Hunnen
unter ihrem König Etzel sich einen
Namen gemacht haben, der sie noch
jetzt in Ueberlieferungen und Märchen
gewaltig erscheinen läßt, so möge
der Name „Deutscher" auf 1000 Jahre
durch Euch in einer Weise betätigt
werden, daß es niemals jemand wagt,
einen Deutschen scheel anzusehen."

(Wilhelm II.)

De même que, mil ans auparavant, les
Huns, sous leur roi Etzel, se sont
fait un nom qui encore aujourd'hui
dans les traditions et dans les contes
leur donne un prestige énorme —
ainsi le nom d'"Allemand' par vous
sera inscrit dans les annales, de sorte
que, pendant mil ans, nul homme osera
regarder de travers un Allemand.

(Guillaume II.)

Evenals 1000 jaren geleden de Hunnen
onder hun koning Attila zich een
naam verworven hebben, die ze nog
tegenwoordig in overleveringen en
sprookjes reusachtig doet lijken, zoo
moge ook de naam „Duitscher" nog
1000 jaar zoo danig bekend worden
dat niemand het ooit weer durft wa-
gen om een Duitscher scheel aan te
kijken.   (Wilhelm II.)

"Just as one thousand years ago the
Huns under their King Etzel made a
great name for themselves, that still
shows powerful traces in traditions
and legends, so also may the name
"German" be made so effective
through you for a thousand years,
that no one in future will ever dare
again to look down upon a German."

(William II.)

Onteerde vrouwenlijken! (Het betreft hier een vrouw uit het Russische Doodenbataillon, die mannelijke soldatenkleeren draagt.)

Violated woman's corpse. (This was the case of a woman belonging to the Russian Battalion of Death, who wore a man's uniform.)

Geschändete Frauenleiche! (Es handelt sich um eine Frau aus dem russischen Todesbataillon, die männliche Soldatenkleider trägt.)

Corps d'une femme à laquelle on a fait violence. (Il s'agit d'une femme du bataillon de mort russe, laquelle porte des habits d'hommes.)

German "heros" in Belgian brothels. ("And German culture shall some day regenerate the world.")

Deutsche „Helden" im belgischen Bordell. („Und es wird am deutschen Wesen einmal noch die Welt genesen.")

Des 'heros' allemands au bordel belgique. (C'est l'esprit allemand qui un jourfera renaitre le monde.)

164

Ein Kulturdokument

Betrieb und Polizei des öffentlichen Hauses in München-Gladbach.

Die zwei Frauen, die das gesamte Personal des öffentlichen Hauses (Gasthausstraße Nr. 2) ausmachen, haben erklärt, daß sie nicht imstande sind, den zahlreichen Besuchern zu genügen, die ihr Haus überschwemmen, vor dem ständig zahlreiche Gruppen ausgehungerter Klienten stehen. Sie erklären, daß sie mit Hinsicht auf den Dienst, den sie ihren belgischen und deutschen Abonnenten schulden, nicht imstande sind, der Division mehr als insgesamt zwanzig Eintritte täglich (jede zehn) zu gewähren. Das Etablissement arbeitet übrigens nicht in der Nacht und hält die Sonntagsruhe strikte ein. Anderseits erlauben die Hilfsquellen der Stadt, wie es scheint, nicht, das Personal zu vermehren. Unter diesen Bedingungen werden zur Vermeidung jeder Unordnung und um von diesen Frauen nicht eine Arbeit zu verlangen, die ihre Kräfte übersteigt, nachstehende Verfügungen getroffen:

Arbeitstage: Alle Tage mit Ausnahme des Sonntags.

Höchstleistung: Jede Frau empfängt je 10 Männer, also 20 für zwei Personen, 120 in der Woche.

Betriebszeit: 5.30 Uhr nachmittags bis 9 Uhr abends. Besuche außerhalb dieser Stunden finden nicht statt.

Tarif: Für einen Aufenthalt von einer Viertelstunde einschließlich Eintritt und Verlassen des Etablissements fünf Mark.

Erfrischungen: Das Haus verkauft keine Getränke. Ein Wartezimmer ist nicht vorhanden. Die Besucher haben sich darin nur zu zweit einzufinden.

Einteilung: Die sechs Tage der Woche sind folgendermaßen zugeteilt:

Montag	1. Bataillon des 164. Regiments
Dienstag . . .	1. Bataillon des 169. Regiments
Mittwoch . . .	2. Bataillon des 164. Regiments
Donnerstag . .	2. Bataillon des 169. Regiments
Freitag	3. Bataillon des 164. Regiments
Samstag . . .	3. Bataillon des 169. Regiments

In jedem dieser Bataillone werden an dem ihm zugewiesenen Tage zwanzig Eintrittskarten, fünf für jede Kompagnie, in den Bureaus der Sergeantmajore ausgelegt. Die Mannschaften, die das Etablissement zu besuchen wünschen, erhalten im Bureau ihres Sergeantmajors eine Karte, die ihnen das Recht der Priorität gibt . . .

Es folgen noch weitere Verfügungen über die „einzelnen", die das Recht haben, einzutreten, wenn die Frauen nicht besetzt sind, und über die Ordnungsmaßnahmen. Es wird namentlich den diensthabenden Offizieren empfohlen, in der Gasthausstraße fleißig nachzusehen, ob alles in Ordnung ist.

Un document de civilisation
Règlement de police pour le commerce dans la maison publique à München-Gladbach.

Les deux femmes dont se compose tous les membres de la maison publique (Gasthaus-Straße Nr. 2) ont déclaré qu'elles ne soient pas capables de satisfaire les clients nombreux qui inondent leur maison, devant laquelle s'amassent continuellement des groupes nombreux de clients affamés. Elles déclarent, qu'en égard au service qu'elles doivent à leurs clients belgiques et allemands, elles étaient hors d'état d'accorder à la division plus de vingt entrées en tout par jour (dix à chacune). L'établissement, d'ailleur, ne travaille pas pendant la nuit et observe exactement le repos du dimanche. D'un autre côté, il semble que les ressources de la ville ne permettent pas d'augmenter le personel. Sous ces circonstances, pour éviter toute sorte de déosdre, et pour ne pas demander de ces femmes un travail qui surpasse leurs forces, on a émis le règlement suivant:

Jours de travail: Tous les jours à l'exception du dimanche.

Maximum de travail: Chaque femme recevra dix hommes (vingt pour les deux), donc 120 par semaine.

Temps de commerce: De cinq heures trente de l'après-midi à neuf heures du soir. Des visites hors de ces heures n'ont pas lieu.

Taxe: Pour le séjour d'un quart d'heure, l'entrée et la sortie y comprises: cinq Mark.

Refraîchissements: L'établissement ne vend pas de boissons. Une salle d'attente n'existe pas. Plus de deux clients ne seront pas admis en même temps.

Ordre de répartition: Les six jours de la semaine sont distribués de la manière suivante:

Lundi	au	1. bataillon du régiment 164
Mardi	„	1. bataillon du régiment 169
Mercredi . . .	,.	2. bataillon du régiment 164
Jeudi	„	2. bataillon du régiment 169
Vendredi . . .	„	3. bataillon du régiment 164
Samedi	„	3. bataillon du régiment 169

Dans chacun de ces bataillons, on réservera au jour fixé vingt cartes d'entrée (cinq pour chaque compagnie) dans les bureaux des sergent-majors. Les hommes de troupe qui désirent fréquenter l'établissement, recevront une carte dans le bureau de leur sergent-major, laquelle leur donne le droit de la priorité . . . Suivent encore d'autres prescriptions pour chacun en particulier qui aura le droit d'entrer quand les femmes ne sont pas occupées, et les règlements de police. On recommande surtout aux officiers du jour de faire des inspections fréquentes dans la Gasthaus-Straße pour constater si tout y en règle.

A cultural document
Rules and Regulations for the control of the brothel in München-Gladbach.

The two women who constitute the entire personnel of the brothel (Gasthausstrasse Nr. 2), have declared that they are not in a position to satisfy the numerous visitors who throng their house, in front of which continuously stand many groups of starving clients. They say that, in consideration of the service that they owe to their German and Belgian clients, they are unable to accept more than 20 visits daily (i. e. 10 each) from the division. Besides, the establishment does not work in the night and strictly maintains Sunday rest. On the other hand, the funds of the town do not permit of an increase in the number of inmates. Under these circumstances, in order to avoid all disorder and so as not to demand of the women a labour that exceeds their capacities, the following orders are hereby issued:

Working days: All days except Sunday.

Maximum work: Each woman receives 10 men, i. e. 20 fo two persons, or 120 in the week.

Hours: 5.30 p. m. to 9. p. m. Visits outside these hours are not permitted.

Tariff: For a stay of a quarter of an hour including entrance into and exit from the establishment, five marks.

Refreshments: The house sells no drinks. There is no waiting-room. Visitors must present themselves in twos.

Apportionment: The six days of the week are divided as follows: —

Monday	. . . .	1st Battalion of the 164th Regiment
Tuesday	. . . .	1st Battalion of the 169th Regiment
Wednesday	. . .	2nd Battalion of the 164th Regiment
Thursday	. . . .	2nd Battalion of the 169th Regiment
Friday	. . . . .	3rd Battalion of the 164th Regiment
Saturday	. . . .	3rd Battalion of the 169th Regiment

In each of these battalions, on the day allotted to it, 20 entrance cards will be laid out in the Sergeant Major's bureau, five for each company. The men who wish to visit the establishment receive in the bureau of their sergeant major a card which gives them the right of priority . . .

There follow other regulations regarding "individuals" who have the right to enter if the women are not occupied, as well as regarding maintenance of order. The officers on duty are recommended to watch the Gasthaus-Strasse observantly, in order to se that all is in order.

Een cultuur-ducument

Bedrijf en politie van het bordeel in München-Gladbach.

De twee vrouwen, die het geheele personeel van het bordeel (Gasthausstr. No. 2) vormen, hebben verklaard, dat zij niet in staat zijn, om nun talrijke bezoekers te voldoen, die hun huis overstroomen en die soms urenlang uitgehongerd voor dit perceel staan. Zij verklaren, dat zij met het oog op den door hun aan hun Duitsche en Belgische abonné's verschuldigden dienst, niet in staat zijn om aan de divisie meer dan te zamen twintig entrée's per dag toe te staan (dus aan ieder tien). Dit etablissement werkt overigens alleen over dag en niet's nachts en handhaaft ook strikt de Zondagsrust. Aan den anderen kant schijnt het, dat een vermeerdering van het personeel onmogelijk is, daar de stedelijke hulpbronnen (geldmiddelen) zulks schijnbaar niet toestaan. Onder deze omstandigheden worden de volgende maatregelen genomen om elke onrust tegen te gaan en om van deze vrouwen geen werk te verlangen, dat hun krachten te boven gaat:

Werkdagen: Alle dagen uitgezonderd Zondags.

Maximum werk: Elke vrouw ontvangt 10 mannen, dus twee personen twintig, 120 in de week, werktijd: 5.30 's namiddags tot 9 uur 's avonds. Buiten dezen tijd hebben er geen bezoeken plaats.

Tarief: Voor een verblijf van een kwartier, inclusief entrée en vertrek uit het etablissement vijf Mark.

Ververschingen: In huis word geen drank verkocht. Een wachtkamer bevindt zich niet in huis. De bezoekers mogen er slechts twee aan twee naar binnen gaan.

Indeeling: De zes dagen der week zijn als volgt verdeeld:

Maandag	. . . .	1ste bataillon van het 164e regiment
Dinsdag	. . . .	1ste bataillon van het 169e regiment
Woensdag	. . .	2de bataillon van het 164e regiment
Donderdag	.	2de bataillon van het 169e regiment
Vrijdag	. . .	3de bataillon van het 164e regiment
Zaterdag	. . . .	3de bataillon van het 169e regiment

In elk bataillon worden op den voor hem bepaalden dag twintig entrékaarten, vijf voor elke compagnie, op de kantoren van de sergeant-majoors neergelegd. De manschappen, die dit etablissement wenschen te bezoeken, krijgen op het bureau van hun sergeant-majoor een kaart, waardoor zij het prioriteitsrecht verkrijgen . . .

Daarna volgen nog andere bepalingen over de „enkelen", die het recht hebben om binnen te komen als de vrouwen niet bezet zijn en en over ordemaatregelen. Aan de dienstdoende officieren wordt namelijk aangeraden om in de Gasthausstraße ijverig te controleeren of ook alles in orde is.

167

Geschändete Wälder.
Des forêts abîmées.
Geschonden bosschen.
Devastated forests.

„Wer hat dich du schöner Wald, aufgebaut so hoch da droben?" (Dtsch. Lied.)
'Belle forêt, de ta taille majustueuse, qui t'as faite naître dans tonte ta
splendeur?' (Chanson allemande.)
"Whose was the hand, O forest fair! That planted thee on those high-
lands there?" (German song.)
„Wie heeft U, o heerlijk woud zoo hoog daarboven opgebouwd?" (Dtsch. lied.)

Destroyed villages.

Zerstörte Dörfer.

Des villages détruits.

169

Getorpedeerd passagierschip.

Torpedoed passenger steamer.

Torpedierter Passagierdampfer.

Bâteau à vapeur détruit par un torpilleur.

Het inwendige van een getorpedeerd passagierschip.

The inside of the torpedoed steamer.

Inneres des torpedierten Dampfers.

Intérieur du bâteau à vapeur détruit.

a) Uit de zeeslag (Skagerak).
Het ondergaande slagschip „Blücher" geeft nog vuur.

a) From the naval battle (Skagerak).
The sinking cruiser „Blücher" still firing.

a) Aus der Seeschlacht (Skagerrak). Der untergehende Kreuzer „Blücher"
feuert noch.

a) De la bataille navale (Skagerak). Le croiseur „Blücher" en coulant bas
fait encore feu.

b) De ondergang van den kruiser.

b) The sinking of the cruiser.

b) Der Untergang des Kreuzers.

b) Le couler bas du croiseur.

Het slot Havrincourt. (Voor het gebruik.)

Havrincourt Castle. (Before use.)

Schloß Havrincourt. (Vor Gebrauch.)

Le château Harincourt. (Avant l'occupation.)

Het slot Havrincourt. (Na het gebruik.)

Havrincourt Castle. (After use.)

Schloß Havrincourt. (Nach Gebrauch.)

Le château d'Havrincourt. (Après l'occupation.)

Fransche soldaten aan het opruimingswerk.

French soldiers in clearing operations.

Französische Soldaten bei Aufräumungsarbeiten.

Des soldats français occupés à des travaux de nettoyage.

Het verwoeste België.

Down - trodden Belgium.

Das zertretene Belgien.

La Belgique écrasée.

Een bom slaat in een huis in.

Bomb attack on a dwelling-house.

Bombeneinschlag in ein Wohnhaus.

L'explosion d'une bombe dans une maison.

„Myn huis is een huis des gebeds, gy echter hebt het tot
een moordenaarskuil gemaakt."

"My house is a house of prayer, but ye have changed it into a murderers'
den".

„Mein Haus ist ein Bethaus, ihr aber habt es zu einer Mördergrube
gemacht."

"Ma Maison est la Maison de prière, mais vous en avez fait une caverne
de voleurs."

Maar waarom heeft dan de lieve God niet eens zyn eigen Godshuizen
beschermd?

But why has Almighty God not even protected his own places of worship?

Aber warum hat denn der liebe Gott nicht mal seine eignen Gotteshäuser
geschützt?

Mais pourquoi le bon Dieu n' a-t-il protigé, pas même ses propres Maisons?

Waar ruwe krachten zinnelos woeden . . .

Where brute force arbitrarily rules . . .

Wo rohe Kräfte sinnlos ,walten . . .

Quand les forces brutes règnent sans raison . . .

Dat is het opbouwende werk van het kapitalisme.

Behold the constructive work of capitalism.

Das ist die Aufbauarbeit des Kapitalismus.

Voilà les travaux de restauration du capitalisme.

Ik antwoordde echter: „Heer, wie zyt gy?" En hy sprak tot my: „Ik ben
Jezus van Nazareth, dien gy vervolgt."

But I answered: "Lord, who art thou?" And he said unto me: "I am Jesus
of Nazareth, whom thou followest."

Ich antwortete aber: „Herr, wer bist Du?" Und er sprach zu mir: „Ich bin
Jesus von Nazareth, den Du verfolgst."

Mais je répondis: "Signeur, qui es tu?" Et il me dit: "Je suis Jesus de
Nazareth, que tu poursuis."

184

In de scholen van New York is n a d e n w e r e l d o o r l o g scherpschieten
als leervak opgenomen!
terwyl de regeeringsvertegenwordigers van alle landen „Vredes" con-
ferenties houden en van „volkeren"-bond en „volkeren"-vrede spreken,
wapenen zy zich op het zelfde moment in alle landen voor een nieuwen
massamoord.

In the New York schools, shooting has been introduced a f t e r t h e W o r l d
W a r! While the representatives of the governments of all countries hold
"Peace Conferences" and speak of "The League of Nations" and "International Peace" they are arming at the same time in all lands for a new
mass murder.

In New Yorker Schulen ist n a c h d e m W e l t k r i e g Scharfschießen
eingeführt worden!
Während die Regierungsvertreter aller Länder „Friedens"-Konferenzen ab-
halten und von „Völker"-Bund und „Völker"-Frieden sprechen, rüsten sie
im selben Augenblick in allen Ländern zum neuen Massenmord.

A p r è s l a g u e r r e u n i v e r s e l l e, on enseigne dans les écoles de
New York le tir à boulets!
En même temps que les représentants des gouvernements de tous pays
tiennent des conférences pour la paix et qu'il parlent de l'Union des peuples
et de la Paix universelle, ils préparent dans tous les pays un massacre
nouveau.

Na den oorlog: de Duitsche kroonprins als hardwerker . . .

After the war: the German Crown Prince as the hardest worker . . .

Nach dem Kriege: Der deutsche Kronprinz als Schwerstarbeiter . . .

Après la guerre: Le Kronprinz d'Allemagne, 'homme de peine . . .

... en de invaliede proletariër by zyn dagelyksche „sport".

... and the war-wounded proletarian at his daily "sport".

... und der kriegsverletzte Proletarier bei seinem täglichen „Sport".

... et le prolétaire mutilé dans la guerre, exécutant son "sport" cotidien.

Na den oorlog: Koning Georg van Engeland aan het zeilen . . .

After the war: King George of England goes in for sailing . . .

Nach dem Kriege: Der König Georg von England treibt Segelsport . . .

Après la guerre: Le roi d'Angleterre, Georg, s'amuse à faire voile . . .

... maar de proletariër???

... but the proletarian???

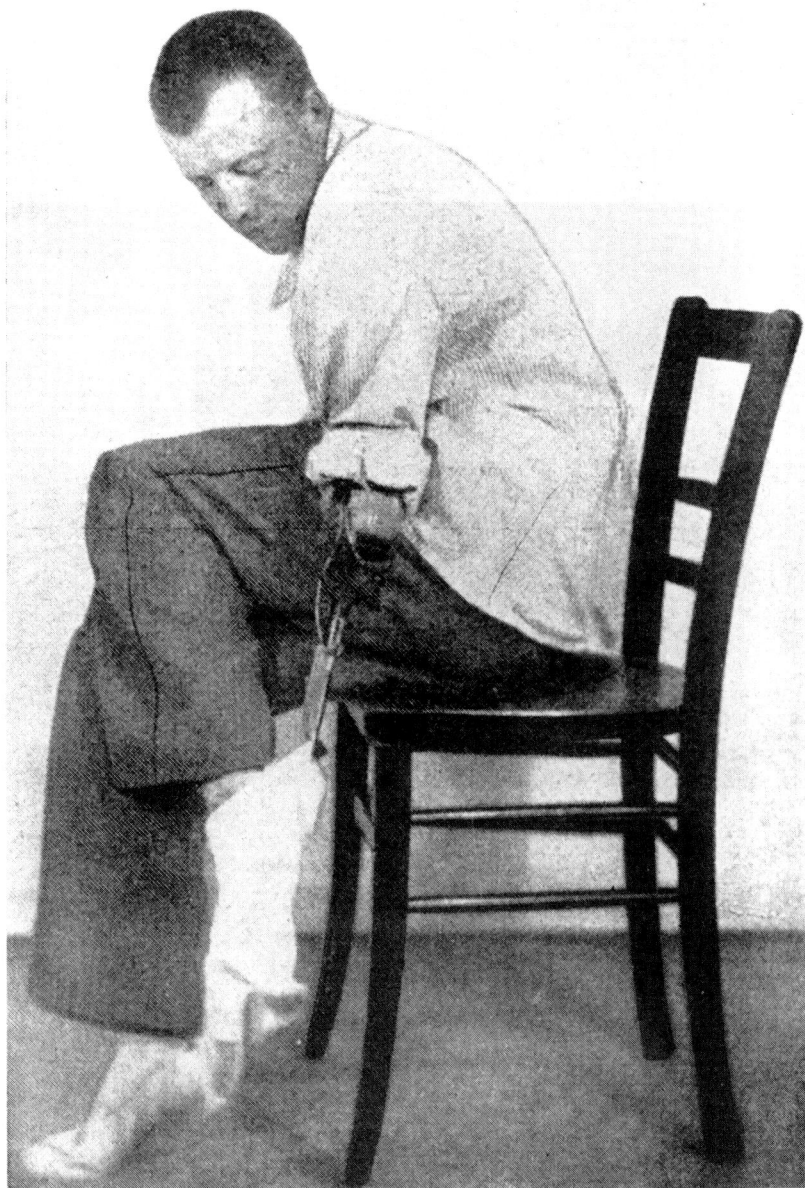

... aber der Proletarier???

... et le prolétaire???

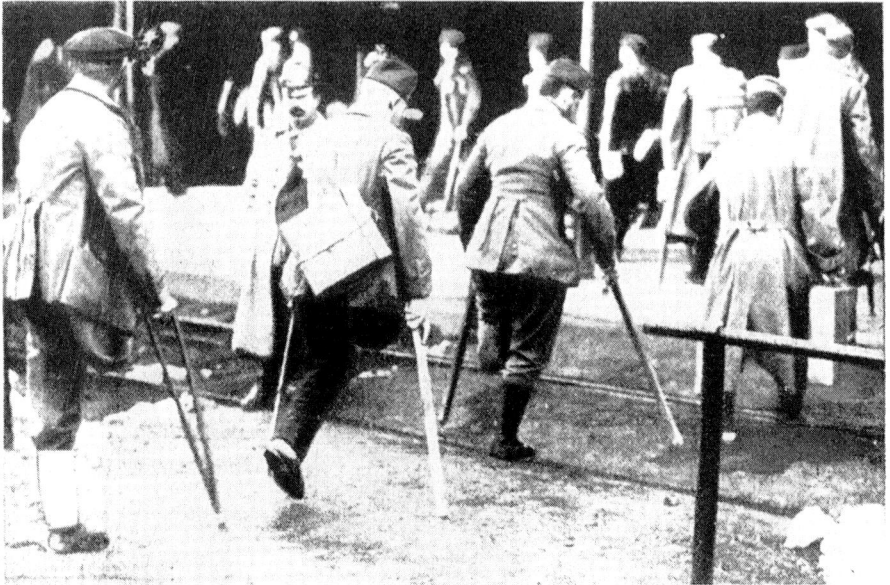

„Was ich bin und was ich habe . . .
"Ce que je suis et ce que je possède . . .
„Wat ik ben en wat ik heb . . .
"All that I am and all that I have . . .

   . . . dank ich dir, mein Vaterland!"

   . . . je te le dois à toi, ma patrie!"

   . . . dat dank ik U, mijn vaderland!"

   . . . I owe to thee, O my country!"

Oorlog den oorlog! „Plundert Gy ten doodgewyden!!!"
Ernst Friedrich (in soldatenuniform) houdt in de Berlijnsche „Siegesallee"
een aanspraak voor Duitsche soldaten en spoort ze tot revolutie aan.

War against! "Rebel!!! O ye that are dedicated to death!"
Ernst Friedrich (in soldier's uniform) speaks to German soldiers in the
Siegesallee in Berlin and calls them out to revolution.

Krieg dem Kriege! „Meutert ihr Totgeweihten!!!"
Ernst Friedrich (in Soldatenkleidung) hält in der Berliner Siegesallee eine
Ansprache an deutsche Soldaten und fordert sie zur Revolution auf.

Guerre à la guerre! "Révoltez — vous! vous, les consacrés à la mort!!!"
Ernst Friedrich (déguise en soldat) dans la Siegesallee à Berlin, fait un
discours à des soldats allemands, en leur demandant de se révolutionner.

192

„De dank des vaderlands is u gewis" —

"You are assured of the gratitude of the Fatherland" —

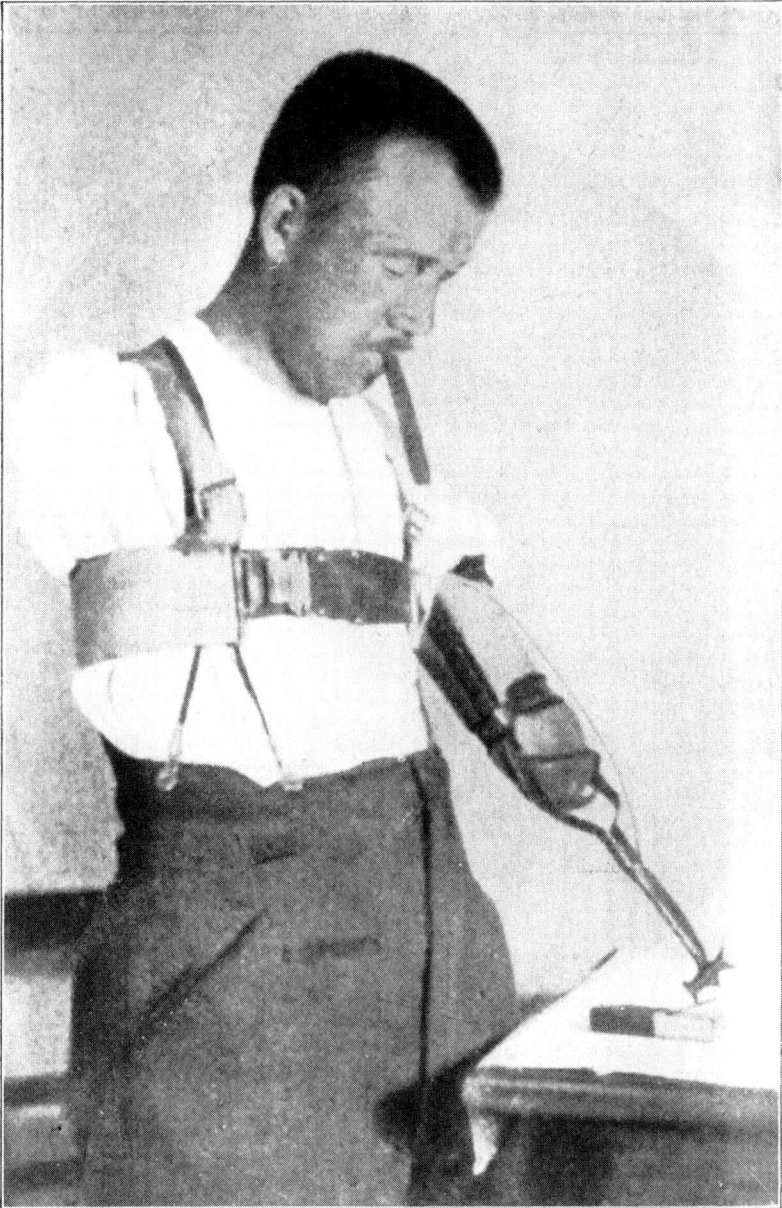

„Des Vaterlandes Dank ist euch gewiß" —

'Le gratitude de la patrie vous est sûre' -

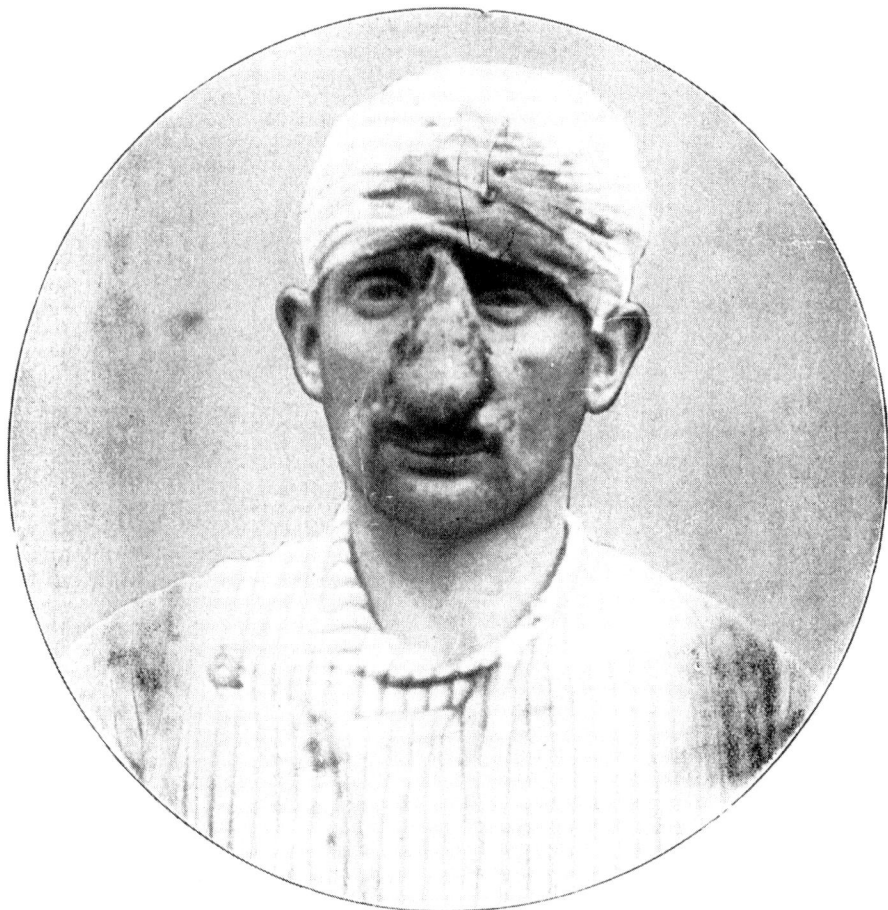

Otto Dorbritz, 27 jaar oud, in Oct. 1918 door een ontploffende myn gewond, hovenlip en neus weggerukt. Vleesch uit voorhoofd, armen en ribben gebruikt voor kunstmatige neus en lip. (12 Operaties.)

Otto Dorbritz, 27 years old, wounded in October 1918 by a mine. Upper-lip and nose torn away. Flesh taken from the forehead, arms and ribs to make artificial nose and lip. (12 operations.)

Otto Dorbritz, 27 Jahre alt, verwundet Oktober 1918 durch Minenwurf Oberlippe und Nase weggerissen. Fleisch aus Stirn, Armen und Rippen zu künstlicher Nase und Lippe entnommen. (12 Operationen.)

Otto Dorbritz, 27 ans, blessé en octobre 1918, par une mine jetée. Nez et lèvre supérieure arrachés. Reconstruits par la chair du front, des bras et des côtes (12 opérations).

Après le bain d'acier: Aujourd'hui encore il y a dans les hôpitaux militaires des soldats horriblement mutilés dans la guerre, soumis toujours à des opérations continuelles. Il y en a qui ont subis de trente à trente cinq opérations, en quelques cas même plus de quarante! Chez bien des milliers entre eux le traitement n'est pas encore fini jusqu'à ce jour Des quantités doivent être nourris d'une manière artificielle.

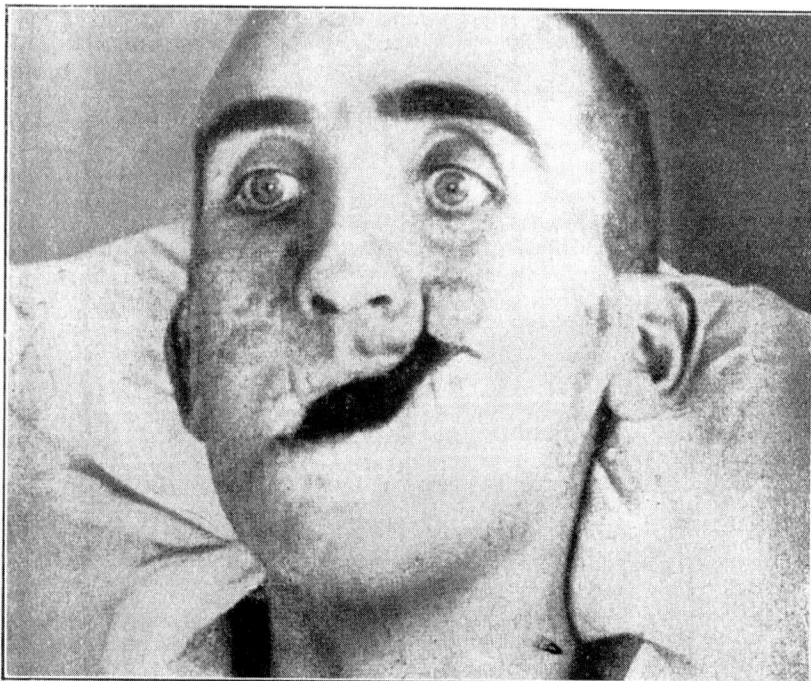

Nach dem Stahlbad: Noch heute liegen in den Lazaretten entsetzlich verstümmelte Kriegsteilnehmer, an denen immer noch herumoperiert wird. Viele dieser unglücklichen Kriegsopfer haben dreißig, fünfunddreißig Operationen, in einzelnen Fällen sogar weit über v i e r z i g O p e r a t i o n e n bisher durchgemacht, und die Behandlung ist bei vielen tausenden heute noch nicht abgeschlossen. Sehr viele müssen künstlich ernährt werden.

Na het staalbad: Nog heden ten dage liggen in de hospitalen ontzettend verminkte soldaten, die altyd weer opnieuw geopereerd moeten worden. Velen van deze ongelukkige slachoffers hebben 30, 35 Operaties, in verschillende gevallen zelfs meer dan 40 operaties doorgemaakt, en de behandeling is by vele duizenden nog niet geeindigd. Zeer velen moeten kunstmatig gevoed worden.

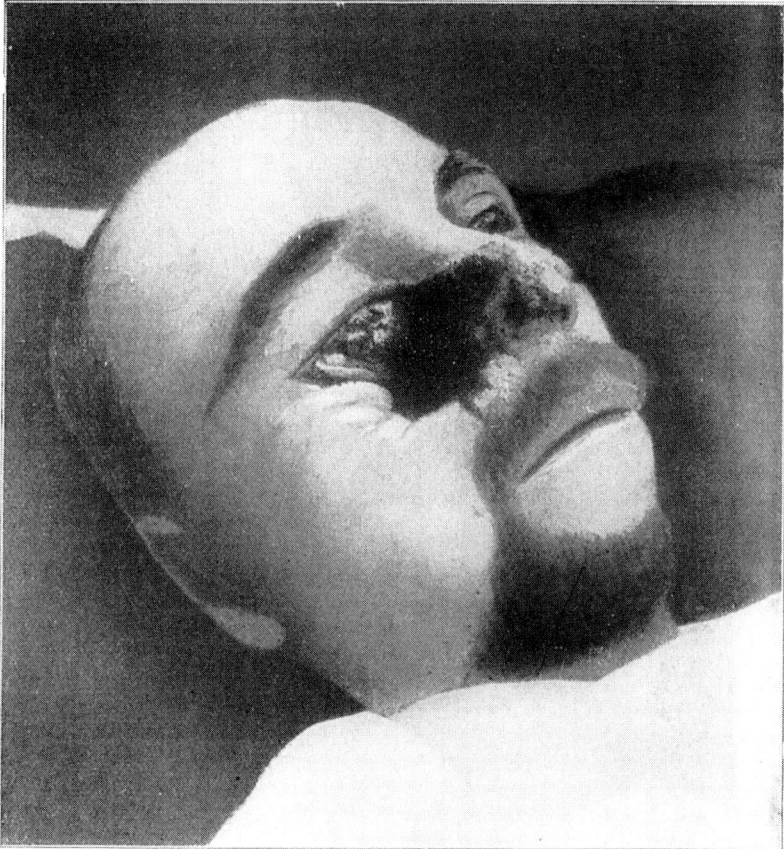

After the steel bath: To the present day are lying in the hospitals gruesomely disfigured soldiers on whom operations are still being performed. Many of these unhappy war victims have undergone thirty, thirty-five and in some cases more than forty operations. In the case of thousands, the medical treatment has not yet been ended. Very many have to be fed artificially.

197

Frans Damman, teekenaar, 44 jaar, gewond Mei 1915. D o o r g r a n a a t -
s p l i n t e r o o r e n o n d e r k a a k m e t g e h e m e l t e w e g g e s l a g e n.
Vervangen met vleesch uit het dybeen. (Tot dusver 30 Operaties.)

Franz Damman, designer, 44 years old. Wounded in May 1915. B y g r a -
n a d e s p l i n t e r s, t h e e a r a n d l o w e r j a w w i t h g u m s w e r e
b l o w n a w a y. Replaced by flesh from upper thigh. (Upto now
30 operations.)

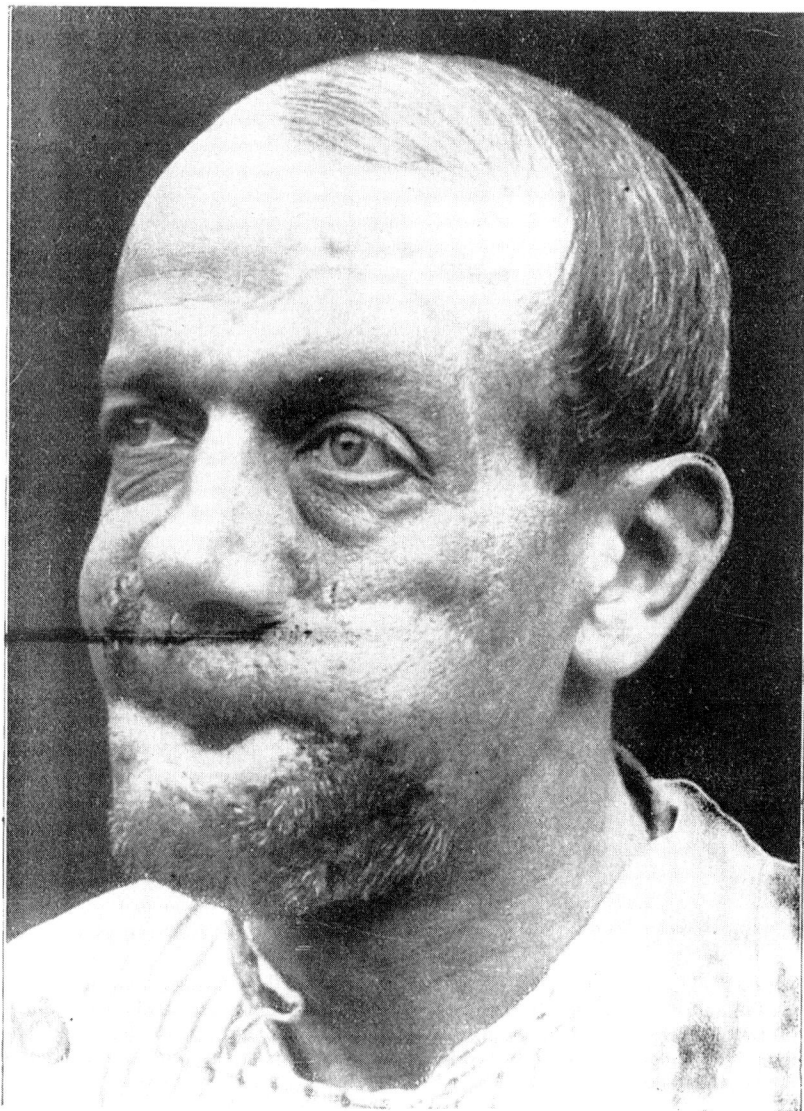

Franz Damman, Zeichner, 44 Jahre. Verwundet Mai 1915. D u r c h
G r a n a t s p l i t t e r O h r u n d U n t e r k i e f e r m i t d e m G a u m e n
a u s g e s c h l a g e n, mit Fleisch aus dem Oberschenkel ersetzt. (Bisher
30 Operationen.)

Franz Damman, dessinateur, 44 ans, blessé en mai 1915 par un éclat d'obus
Oreille et mâchoire inférieure détruites; reconstruites de chair prise de
198   la cuisse supérieure. (Jusque là 30 opérations.)

Karl Marzahn, yzerwerker, 37 jaar, gewond 26. Oct. 1918. O n d e r k a a k, t a n d e n e n t o n g w e g g e r u k t, gerepareerd met vleesch uit hoofd en borst.

Karl Marzahn, iron planer, 37 years old. Wounded 26. 10. 1918. L o w e r j a w, t e e t h a n d t o n g u e t o r n a w a y. Patched up with flesh from head and chest.

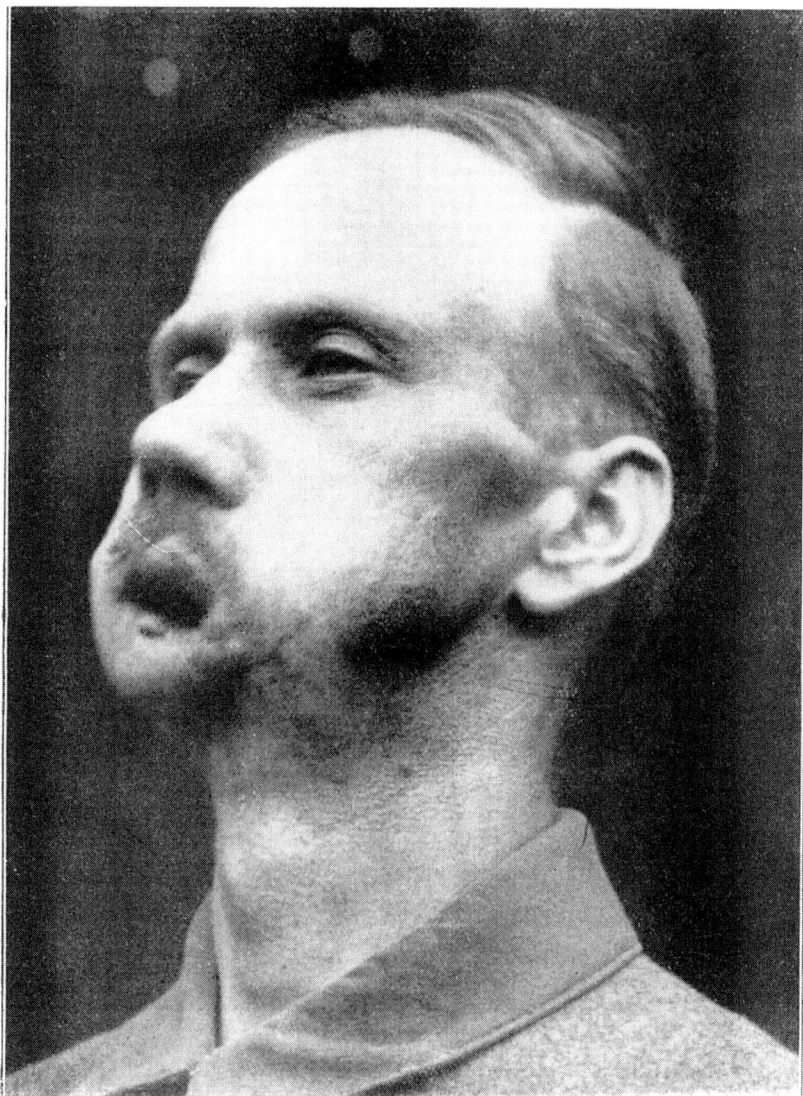

Karl Marzahn, Eisenhobler, 37 Jahre. Verwundet 26. 10. 1918. U n t e r - k i e f e r, Z ä h n e u n d Z u n g e a b g e r i s s e n, ausgeflickt mit Fleisch aus Kopf und Brust.

Karl Marzahn, raboteur de fer, 37 ans. Blessé le 26 octobre 1918. Mâchoire inférieure, dents et langue arrachées. Reconstruites de chair prise de la tête et de la poitrine.

Landarbeider, 36 jaar oud, gewond in 1917. Neus en linker wang verwangen met vleesch, uit hoofd borst en arm. (20 Operaties.)

Agricultural worker, 36 years of age. Wounded 1917. Nose and left cheek restored with flash from head, beast and arm. (20 operations.)

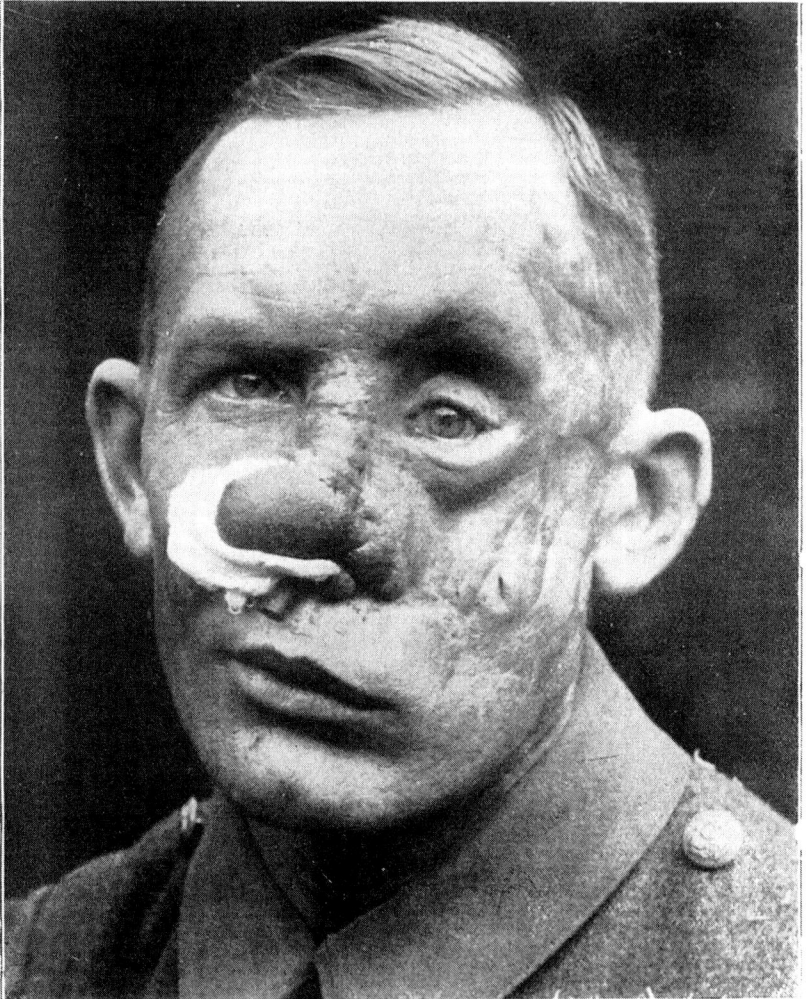

Landwirtschaftlicher Arbeiter, 36 Jahre alt. Verwundet 1917. Nase und linke Wange ersetzt aus Fleisch von Kopf, Brust und Arm. (20 Operationen.)

Agriculteur, 36 ans, blessé en 1917. Le nez et la joue gauche restitués par la chair de la tête, de la poitrine et du bras. (20 opérations).

Eenige invalieden weigerden nadere byzonderheden. Andere gewonden, in het byzonder de afschuwelyk verminkten lieten zich niet fotograveeren, om dat zy vreesden, dat hunne familieleden, die hen tot dusver nog niet hebben teruggezien, by den aanblik von hun ellende zouden bezwymen of zich voor altyd vol afschuw en ontzetting van hen zouden afkeeren.

Some war cripples refused information, other wounded, particularly those gruesomely mutilated, did not allow themselves to be photographed, as they feared that their relatives who had not seen them again, would either collapse at the sight of their misery, or would turn away for ever from them in horror and disgust.

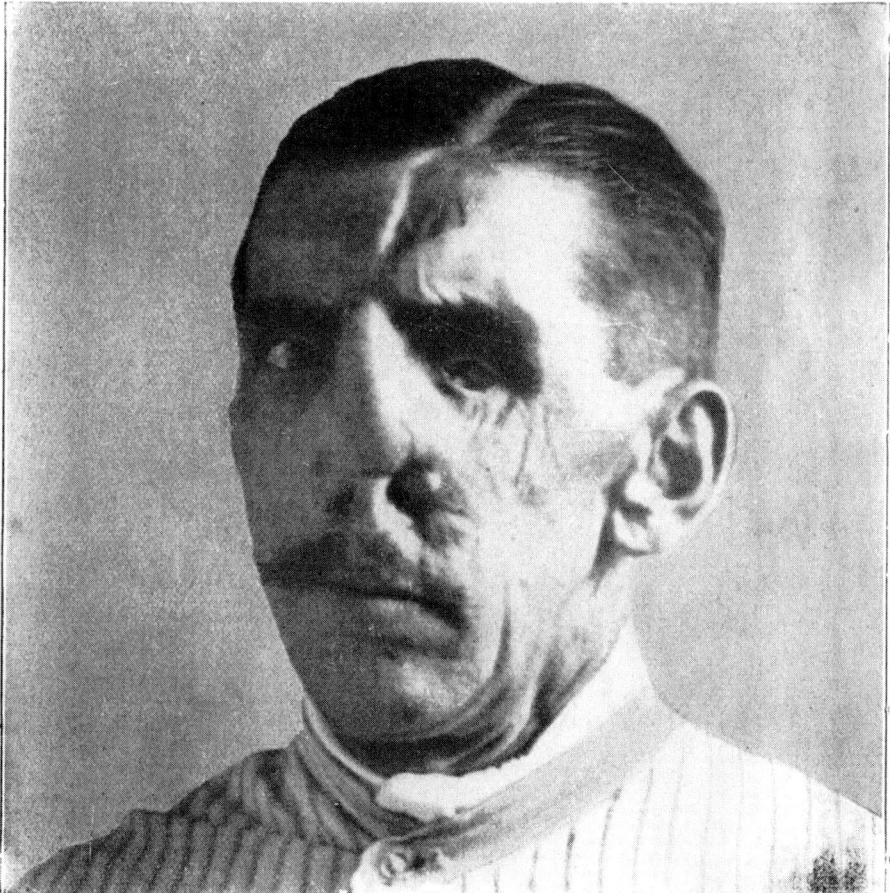

Einige Kriegskrüppel verweigerten nähere Angaben, andere Verletzte, insbesondere die ganz grauenhaft verstümmelten, ließen sich nicht photographieren, weil sie fürchteten, daß ihre Angehörigen, die sie bisher noch nicht wiedergesehen haben, beim Anblick ihres Elends zusammenbrechen oder sich für immer voll Ekel und Entsetzen von ihnen abwenden würden.

Quelques uns des estropiés de guerre refusaient de faire des indications spéciales. D'autres, surtout ceux avec les mutilations les plus affreuses, ne souffraient pas qu'on les photographiât, craignant que leur parenté, qui jusque là ne les avait pas encore revus, à l'aspect de leur misère puissent s'écrouler ou bien se détourner d'eux à jamais, repoussé de dégoût et d'épouvante.

Een echte gave des hemels is het licht der oogen.
(Granatsplitter reet in 1915 het geheele gezicht weg. Blind.)

A noble gift of Heaven is the light of the eye. (Granade
splinters tore away his eys, in 1915.)

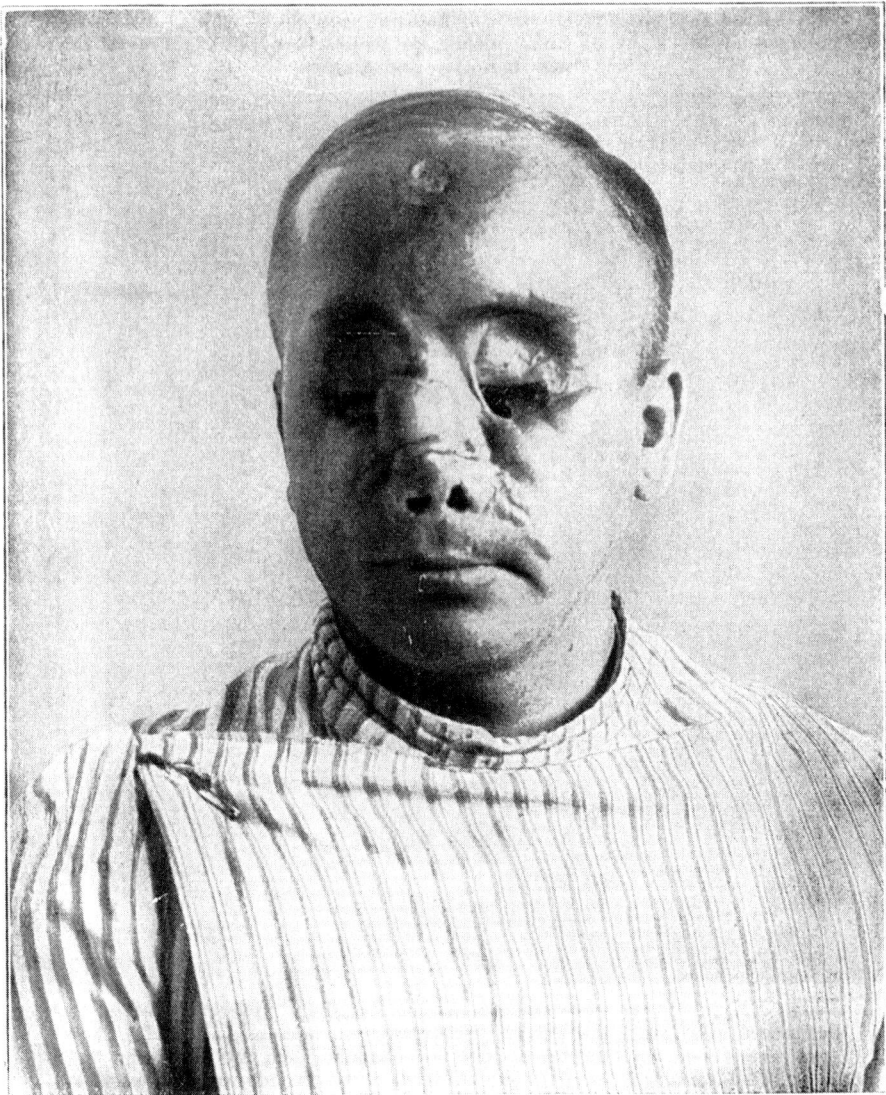

Eine edle Himmelsgabe ist das Licht des Auges.
(Granatsplitter riß 1915 beide Augen und Nase weg.)

Ah! quel don céleste que la lumière du jour! (Par des éclats
d'obus, en 1915, les deux yeux et le nez arrachés.)

Een 25 jarige landbouwer, in 1916 door granaatsplinter gewond, gezicht uiteengerukt, door tallooze operaties vervangen.

A twenty-five year old peasant wounded in 1916 by granade fragments. Mutilated face restored after numberless operations.

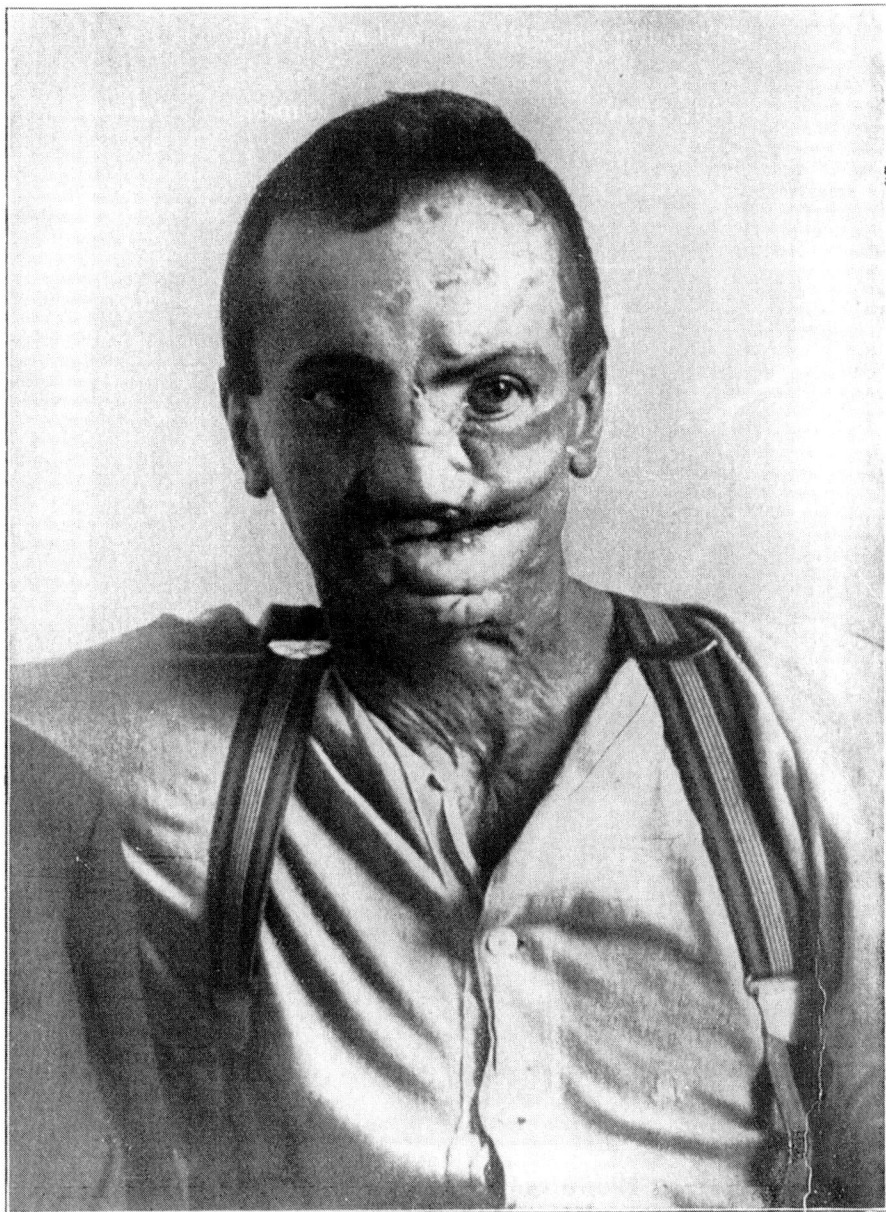

Ein 25 jähriger Landwirt, verwundet 1916 durch Granatsplitter. Zerrissenes Gesicht durch zahllose Operationen ersetzt.

Un cultivateur (25 ans), blessé en 1916. Figure déchirée par éclats d'obus, restituée par des opérations nombreuses.

Spoorwegarbeider. Mond en rechterhand weg. Onderkaak
verbryzeld.

Railwayman. Mouth and right hand torn away. Lower jaw gone.

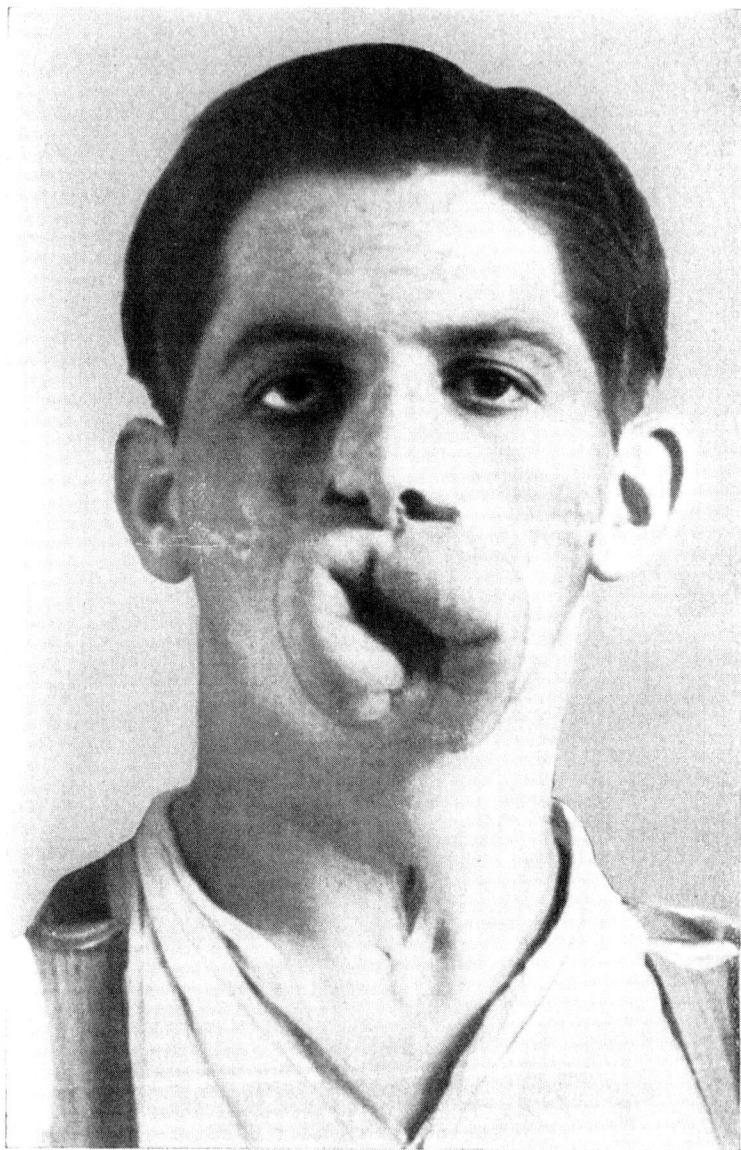

Eisenbahner. Mund und rechte Hand ab. Unterkiefer
zerrissen.

Ouvrier aux chemins de fer. La bouche et la main droite arrachées.
La mâchoire déchirée.

Zooals deze ongelukkigen moeten vele duizenden kunstmatig gevoed
worden.

Many thousands have to be a r t i f i c i a l l y f e d, like this unhappy man.

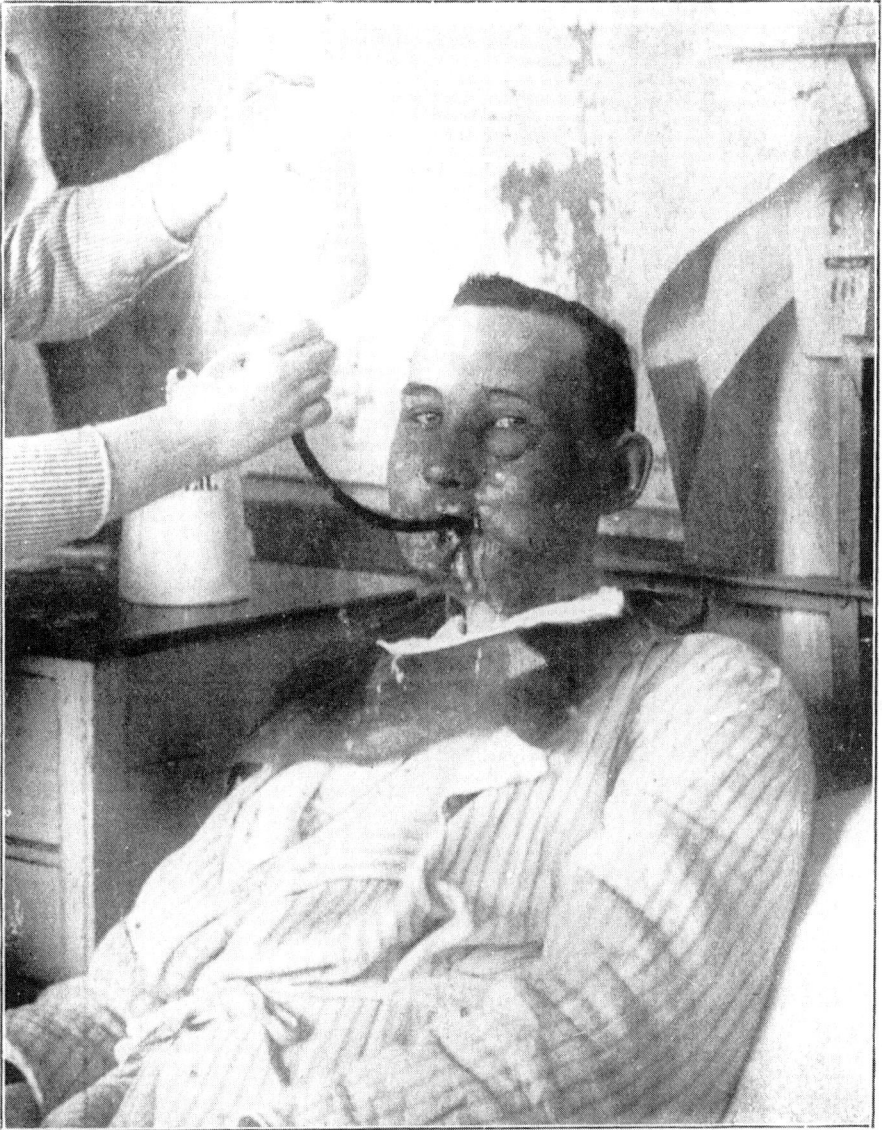

Wie dieser Unglückliche, müssen viele Tausende k ü n s t l i c h e r n ä h r t
werden.

De la même manière artificielle que ce malheureux-ci, bien des milliers
doivent être nourris.

Neus weggerukt en ervangen door vleesch uit dybeen. Voorhoofd
en mond gekwetst.

Nose blown away and restored with flesh from upper thigh. Forehead
and mouth wounded.

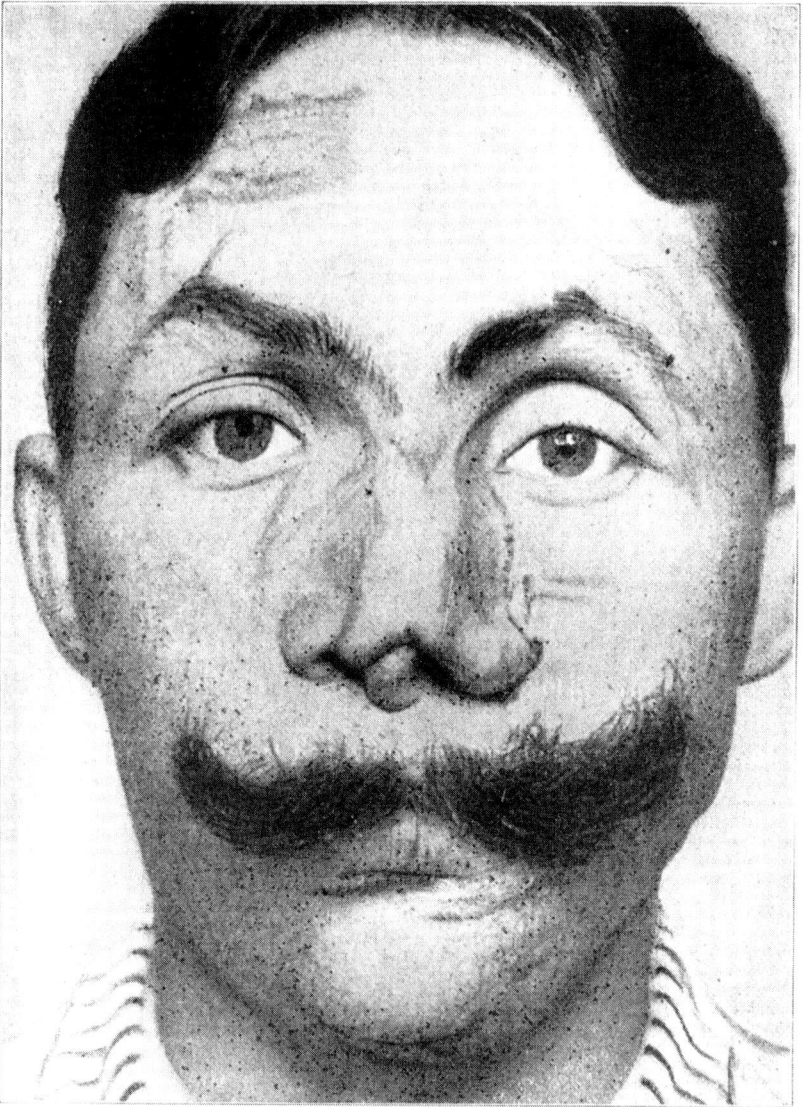

Nase weggerissen und ersetzt aus Fleisch vom Oberschenkel. Stirn
und Mund verletzt.

Le nez arraché et reconstruit par la chair de la cuisse.
Le front et la bouche blessés.

Soldaat D. Wang, mond en tanden weggeschoten. Gewond 27. Dec. 1914.

Corporal D. Cheek, mouth and teeth torn away. Wounded
27. 12. 1914.

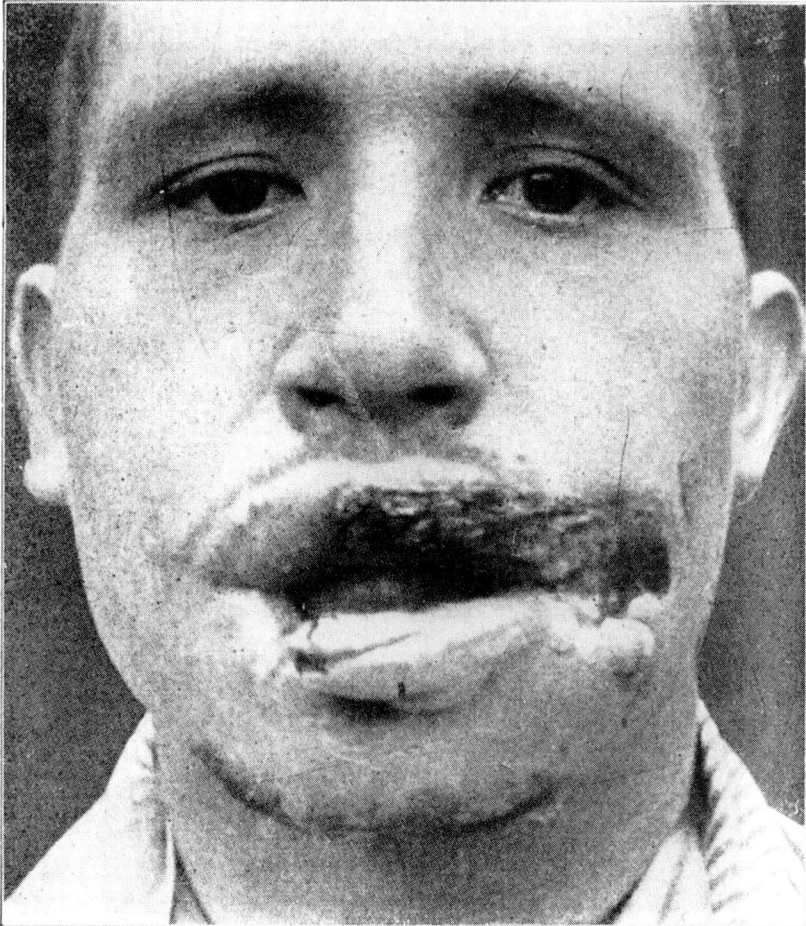

Gefreiter D. Wange, Mund und Zähne weggerissen.
Verwundet 27. Dezember 1914.

Soldat de première classe D. La bouche et les dents arrachées.
Blessé le 27. décembre 1914.

Soldaat F. Onderkaak en tanden uitgeslagen. Verwond 26. Sept. 1914.
Behandeling nog steeds niet ten einde.

Corporal F. Lower jaw and teeth blown away. Wounded 26. 9. 1914.
Treatment not yet ended.

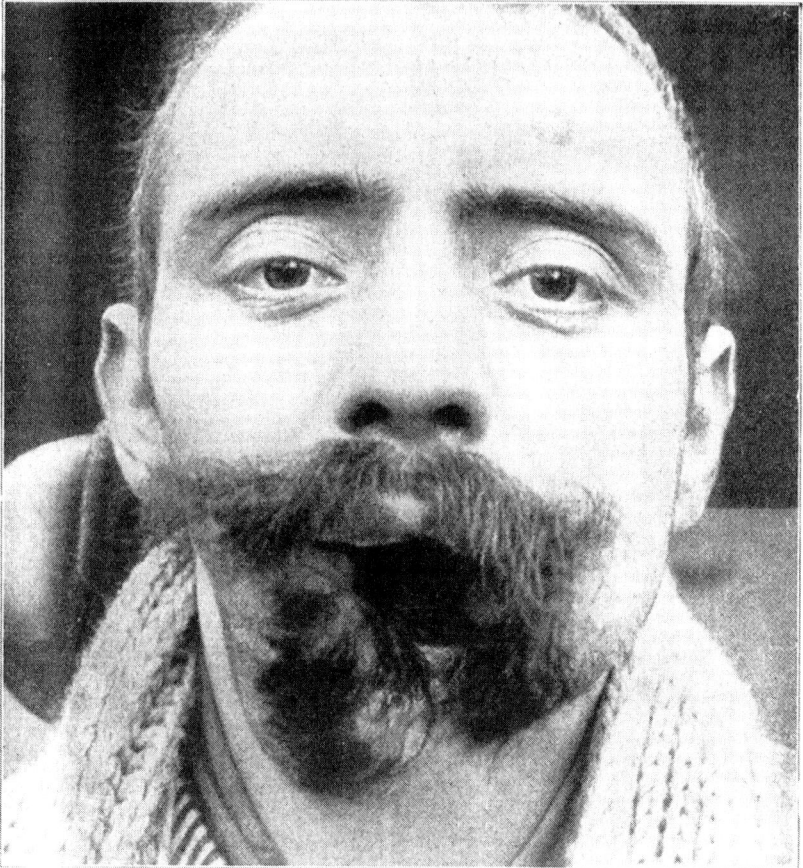

Gefreiter F. Unterkiefer und Zähne ausgeschlagen.
Verwundet 26. 9. 1914. Behandlung noch nicht abgeschlossen.

Soldat de première classe F. La mâchoire inférieure et les dents démolées
Blessé le 26. septembre 1914. Traitement pas encore fini.

Er zijn alleen in Duitschland nog altijd 48 000 verpleegden in hospitalen,
die afgescheiden van de wereld, ver van hun familie, ver van vrienden en
bekenden, voortleven in de hoop dut zy wellicht na jaren een eenigszins
menschelyk uiterlyk zullen terugkrygen.

In Germany alone there are still 48 000 hospital inmates who are
totally cut off from the world and drag on their existences far from their
families and friends and relatives, in the hope that they may perhaps after
years again acquire the appearance of human beings.

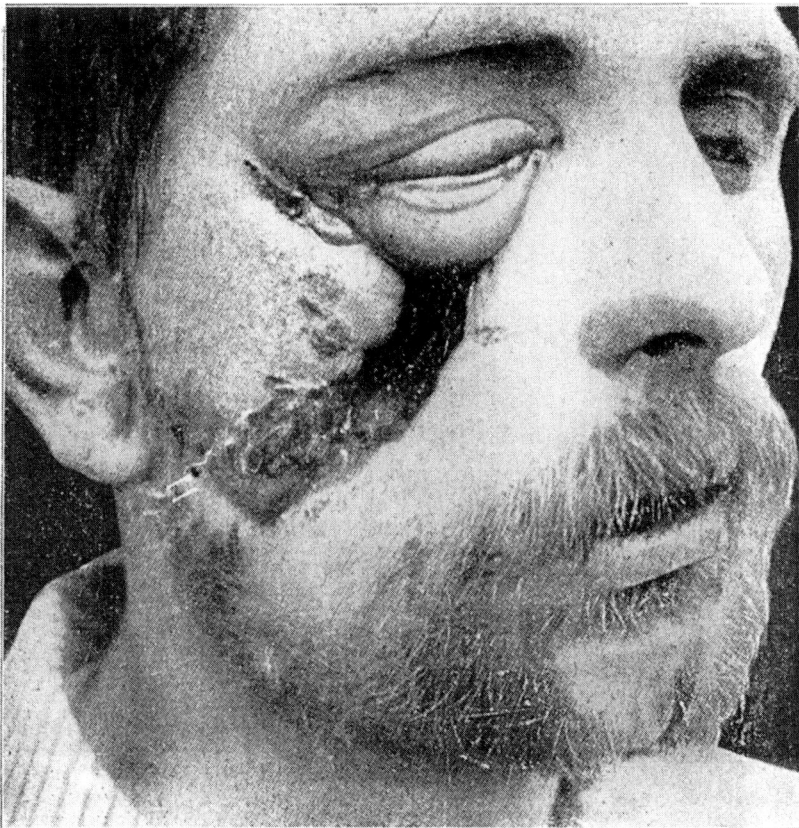

Es gibt allein in Deutschland immer noch 48 000 Lazarettinsassen, die welt-
abgeschieden, fern von ihrer Familie, fern von Freunden und Bekannten
dahinleben in der Hoffnung, daß sie vielleicht nach Jahren ein menschen-
ähnliches Aussehen wieder erhalten.

Rien qu'en Allemagne, il y a toujours 48 000 habitants d'hôpitaux militaires, végétant loin du monde, loin de leurs familles, de leurs amis et
connaissances, dans l'espoir vague que peut-être, après de longues années,
ils réussissent à regagner des dehors humainement possibles.

Reservist St. R. gewond 16. Mei 1915.

Reserve St. R. Wounded 16. 5. 1915.

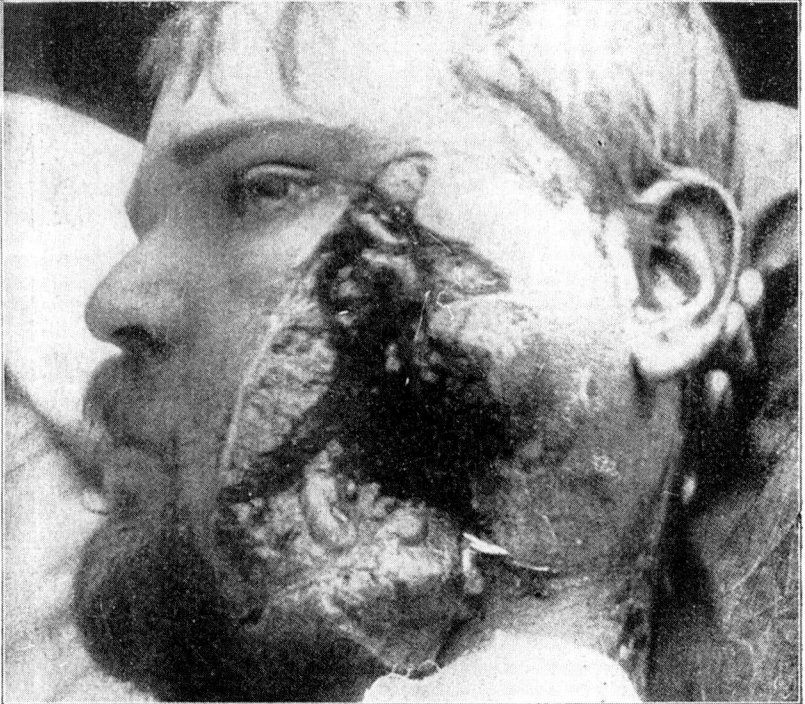

Ersatzreservist St. R. Verwundet 16. 5. 1915.

Homme de la réserve de recrutement, St. R. E., blessé le 16 mai 1915.

Onderofficier D., gewond 20. Mei 1920. Behandeling nog niet geeindigd.

Non-commissioned officer D. Wounded 20. 5. 1915. Treatment not yet ended.

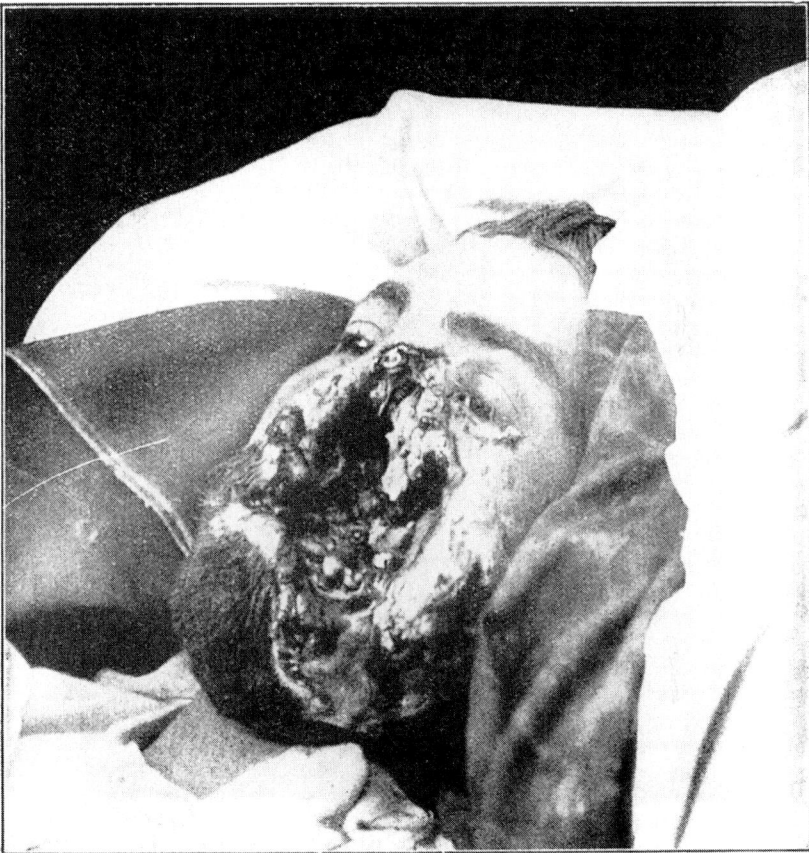

Unteroff. D., verwundet 20. 5. 1915. Behandlung noch nicht abgeschlossen.

Sous-officier D., blessé le 20 mai 1915. Traitement pas encore fini.

Reservist S. thans nog in operatieve behandeling.

Reserve S., still undergoing operations.

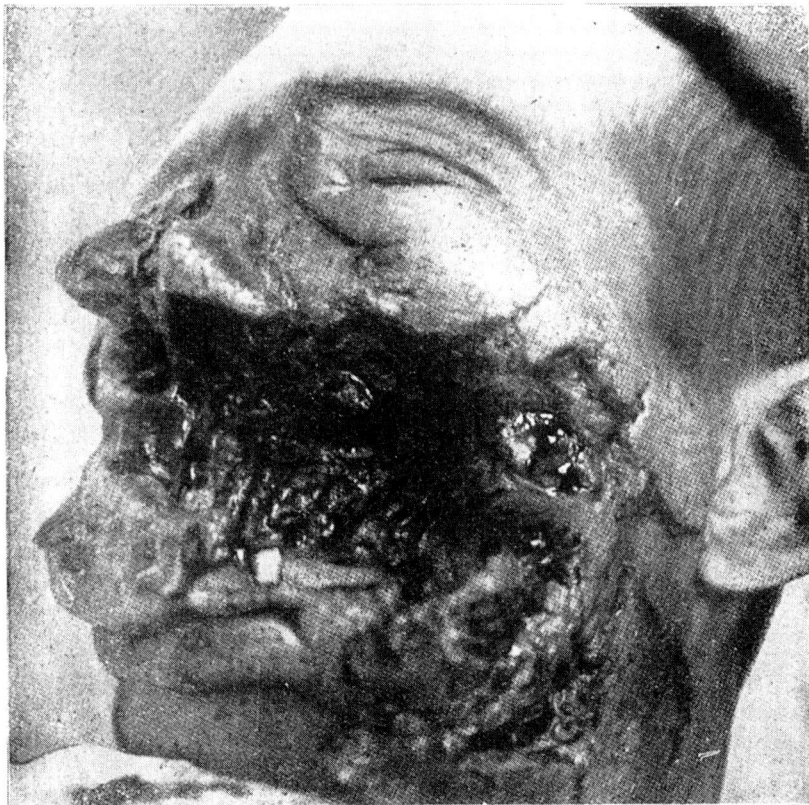

Ersatzreservist S. heute noch in operativer Behandlung.

Homme de la réserve de recrutement, S. Encore aujourd'hui en traitement opératif.

Musketier R. gewond 27. Sept. 1914. Behandeling nog niet ten einde.

Fusilier R. Wounded 27. 9. 1914. Still under traetment.

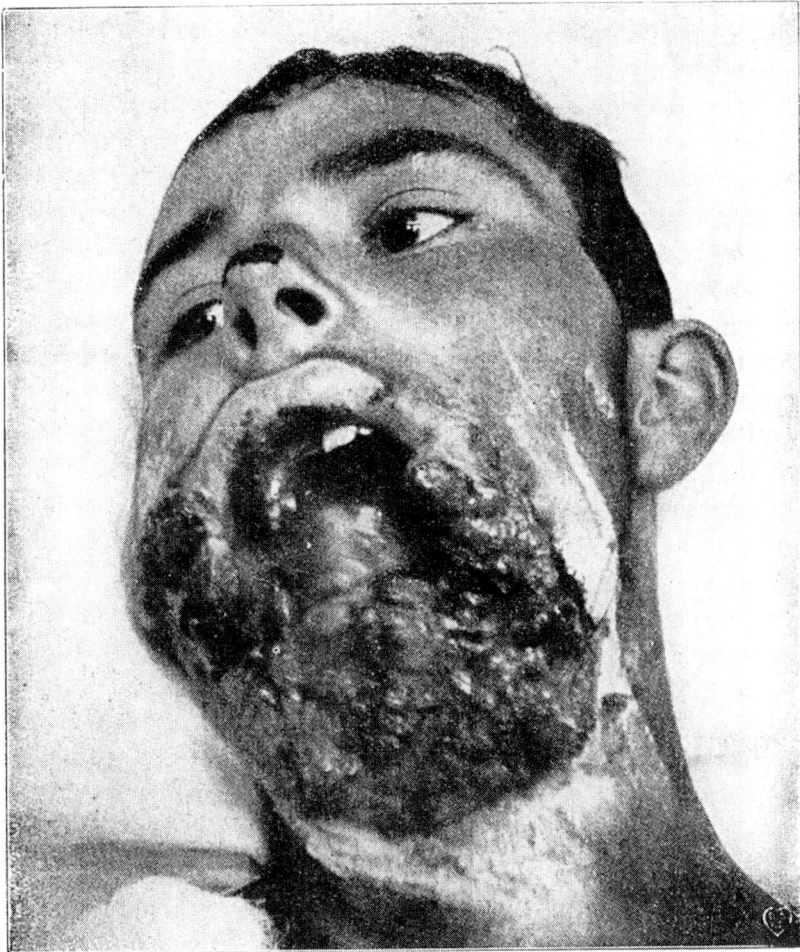

Füsilier R., verwundet 27. 9. 1914. Behandlung noch nicht abgeschlossen.

Fusilier R., blessé le 27. septembre 1914. Traitement pas encore fini.

De tangen van den doktor.

The doctor's forceps.

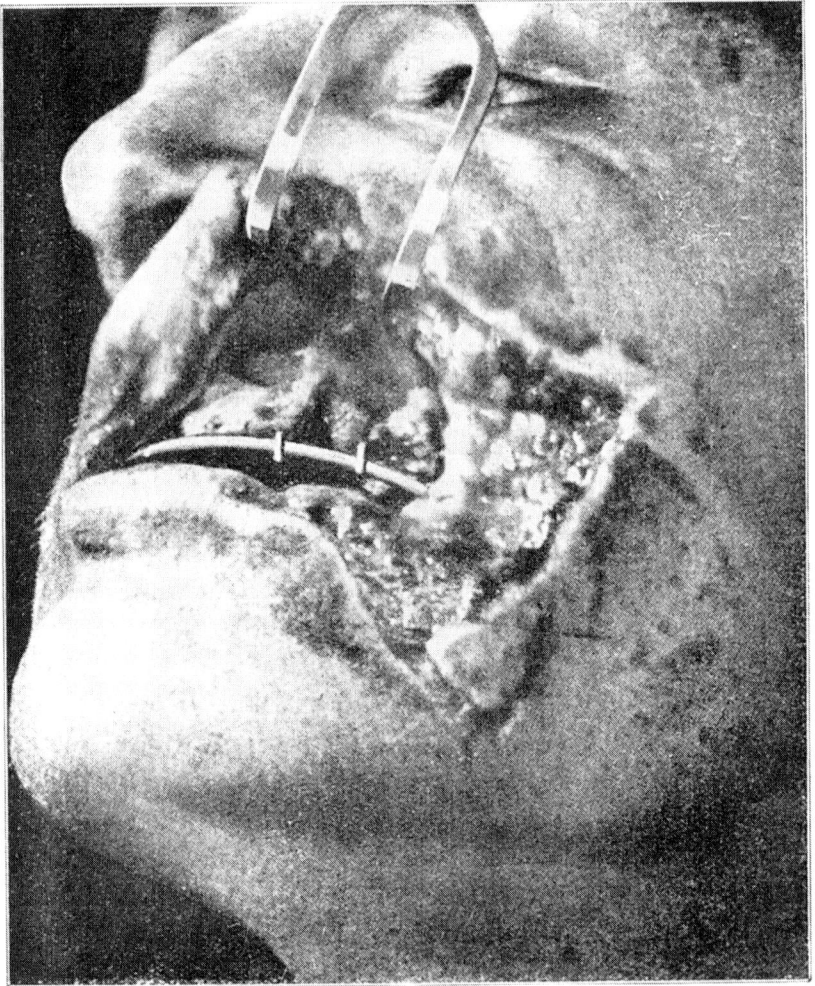

Die Zangen des Arztes.

Les tenailles du médecin.

Tal van operaties moeten by vol bewustzyn, (zonder eenige narvose of pynverdoovende middelen) worden uitgevoerd.

Many operations have to be carried out in full consciousness (without any narcotic or anaesthetic).

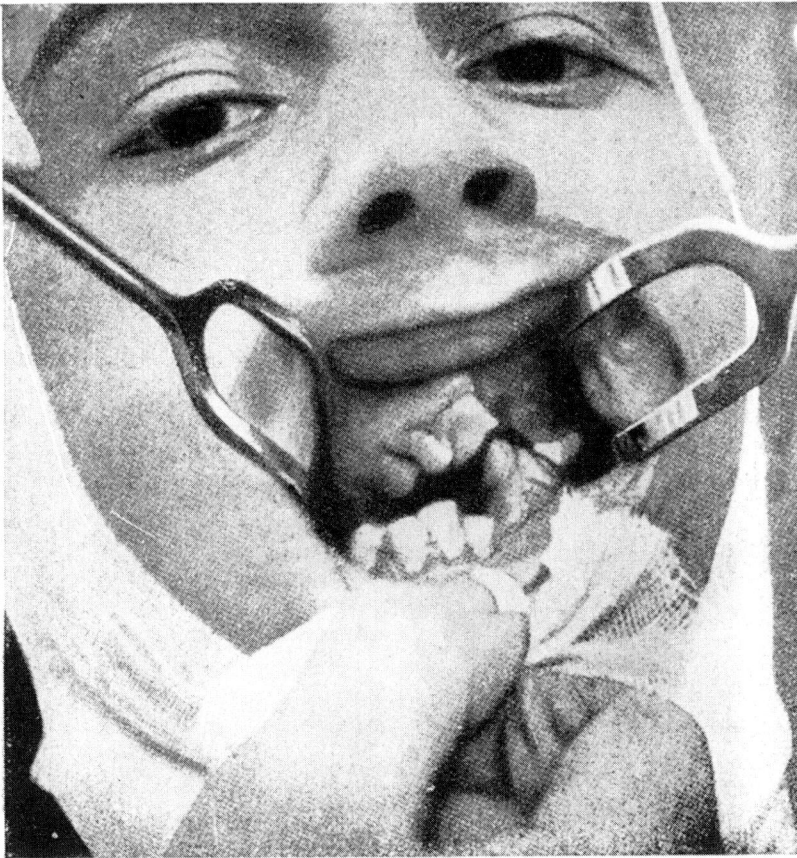

Viele Operationen müssen bei vollem Bewußtsein (ohne jede Narkose oder schmerzlindernde Betäubung) ausgeführt werden.

Beaucoup d'opérations doivent être faites en pleine connaissance du patient, (sans aucune narcose ou médicament calmant la douleur).

„De oorlog bekomt my als een kuur" (Hindenburg).

„War agrees with me like a stay at a health resort." (Hindenburg.)

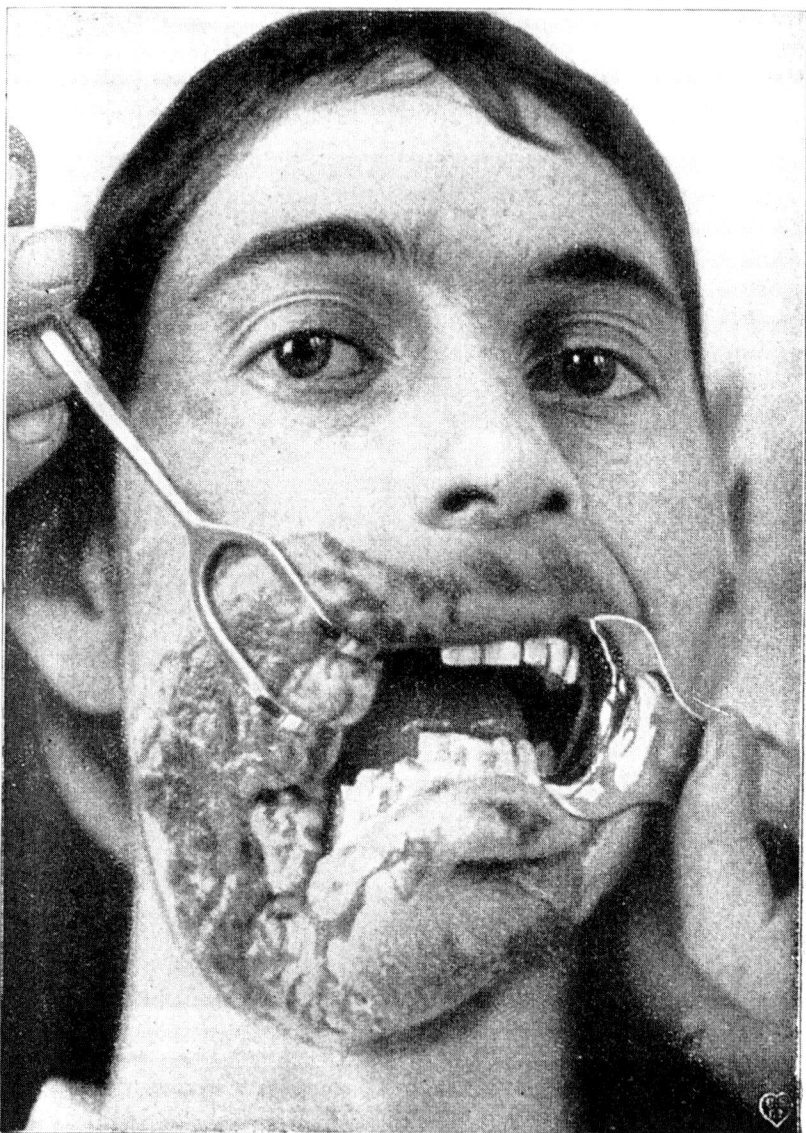

„Der Krieg bekommt mir wie eine Badekur." (Hindenburg.)

'La guerre est pour moi un traitement d'eaux minérales.' (Hindenburg.)

216

De kuur der proleten! Byna het heele gezicht weggeschoten.

The "health resort" of the proletarian. Almost the whole face
blown away.

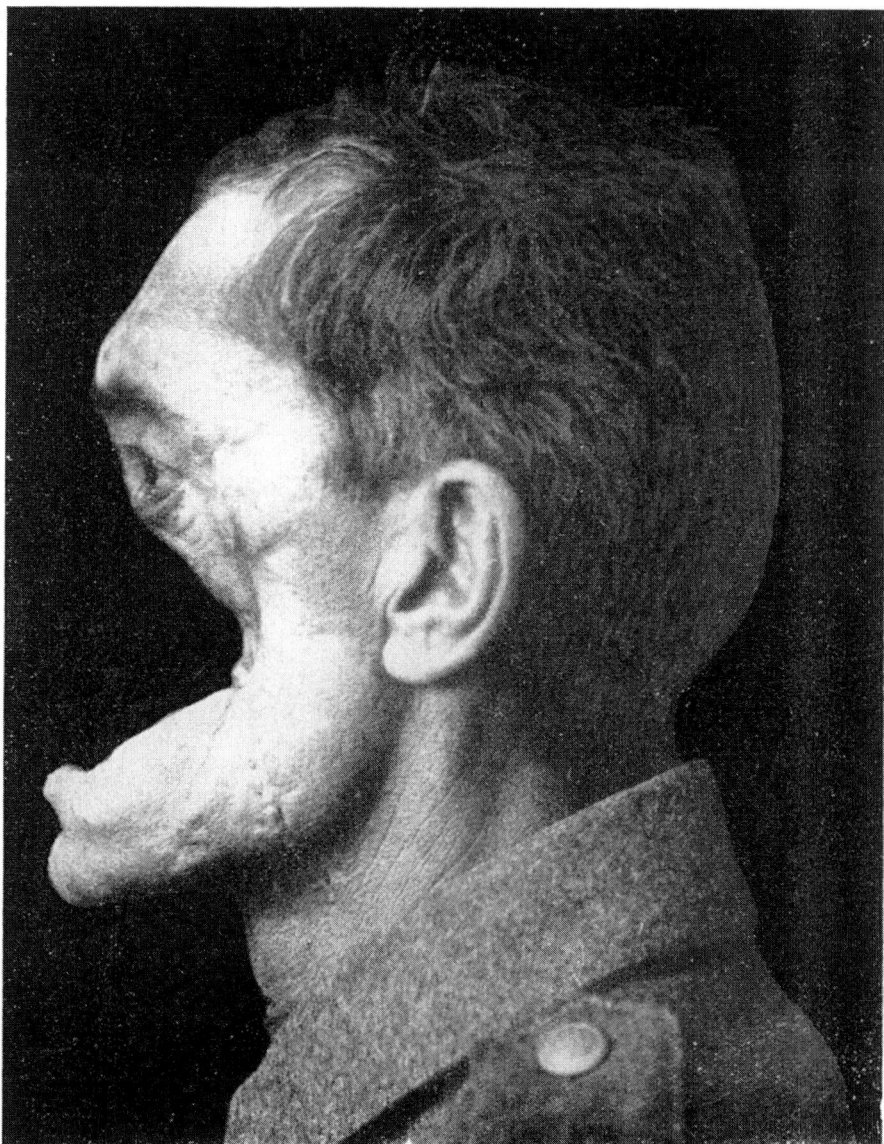

Die Badekur der Proleten: Fast das ganze Gesicht weggeschossen.

Le 'traitement d'eaux minérales' des prolétaires: presque la figure entière arrachée.

Het woord: K a m e r a d e n is in het opschrift door de Franschen met
zwarte verf onzichtbaar gemaakt.

The word C o m r a d e s in the inscription made invisible with black paint
by the French.

Das Wort: K a m e r a d e n ist in der Aufschrift durch die Franzosen mit
schwarzer Farbe unsichtbar gemacht.

A l'inscription le mot: c a m a r a d e s est fait invisible par les Français
à moyen de couleur noire.

Het kerkhof van Nesle. Door de Franschen vernielde Duitsche grafsteenen.

The churchyard in Nesle. Grave-stones destroyed by the French.

Der Kirchhof von Nesle. Durch die Franzosen vernichtete deutsche Grabsteine.

La cimetière de Nesle. Des pierres tumulaires allemandes détruites par les Français.

Het kerkhof van Nesle. (De Duitsche grafkruisen zyn alle omvergeworpen,
de Fransche zyn laten staan en met kransen versierd.)

The churchyard in Nesle. (The German grave-stones all thrown down, the
French ones left standing and crowned with wreaths.)

Der Kirchhof von Nesle. (Die deutschen Grabkreuze sind sämtlich um-
geworfen, die französischen stehen gelassen und bekränzt.)

La cimetière de Nesle. (Les croix des tombeaux allemands sont toutes ren-
versées; celles des tombeaux français sont laissées intactes et couronnées
de guirlandes.)

220

Het kerkhof van Nesle.

The churchyard in Nesle.

Der Kirchhof von Nesle.

La cimetière de Nesle.

Grondig „werk".

Thorough „work".

Gründliche „Arbeit".

Un 'travail' comme il faut.

Met moedwil beschadigd inschrift.

Maliciously destroyed inscription.

Den ist der Nachruhm.
von
gefallenen Kameraden
zu ihrer Ehre
durch dieses Denkmal
das XIV. Reserve Korps
191.. – 191..

Mutwillig beschädigte Aufschrift.

Inscription abimée à dessein.

Grafmonument op het kerkhof van Peronne. De naam van het regiment is met een byl weggehouwen.

Epitaph in the churchyard in Peronne. The name of the regiment is hewn away with an axe.

Grabmonument auf dem Kirchhof in Peronne. Der Name des Regiments ist mit einem Beil weggehauen.

Monument funéraire à la cimetière de Péronne. Le nom du régiment est enlevé à coups de hache.

Ein deutsches Grabmonument auf dem Kirchhof in Peronne. Man sieht hier deutlich, wie mit einem Beil die Aufschrift: „Hier ruhen deutsche Soldaten" weggemeißelt ist. (Die Spuren der Beilhiebe sind noch deutlich zu sehen. Darunter ist das Wort „Boches" eingekratzt.)

Kerkhof van Mesnil. Een scherts van de Franschen.

Churchyard in Mesnil. A small French joke.

Kirchhof von Mesnil. Ein kleiner Franzosenscherz.

Le cimetière de Mesnil. Une petite plaisanterie des Français.

A l'image au page 225.

Un monument funéraire allemand au cimetière de Peronne. On y voit clairement que l'inscription: 'Ici reposent des soldats allemands' est envelée. (Les traces des coups de hache sont distinctement visibles. Au dessous le mot 'Boches' est gravé.)

Text zum Bild auf Seite 225.

Een Duitsch grafmonument op het kerkhof van Peronne. Men ziet hier duidelyk, hoe met een byl het inschrift: „Hier rusten Duitsche soldaten" weggebeiteld is. (De spoen van de bylhouwen zyn nog duidelyk te zien. Daaronder is het woord „Boches" ingekrast.)

Text to picture on p. 225.

German epitaph in the churchyard in Peronne. It can be clearly seen how the inscription, "Here lie German soldiers", was hewn away with an axe. (The traces of the axe-strokes can still be clearly seen. Underneath, the word „Boches" scratched in.)

„De edelste deugden van den mensch ontwikkelen zich in den oorlog!"
(Graaf Moltke.)

In den oorlog der spanijarden tegen de, om hunne onafhankelykheid strydende marokkanen, hebben Spaansche soldaten den gevangen het hoofd abgeslagen en opgespietst.

"The noblest virtues of men are developed in war!" (Count Moltke.)

In the war of the Spaniards against the Maroccans fighting for their independence, the Spanish soldiers cut off the heads of their prisoners and stuck them on poles.

„Die edelsten Tugenden der Menschen entfalten sich im Krieg!
(Graf Moltke.)

Im Krieg der Spanier gegen die ihre Unabhängigkeit verteidigenden Marokkaner haben spanische Soldaten den Gefangenen die Köpfe abgeschlagen und aufgespießt.

'Les vertues d'hommes les plus nobles florissent dans la guerre'.
(Citat du comte Moltke.)

Pendant la guerre des Espagnols contre les Marocains défendants leur indépendence, des soldats espagnols ont coupé et enferré les têtes aux prisonniers.

15*

Gedenktafel uit marmer voor den hoogen officier . . .

Memorial stone of marble for the high officer . . .

Gedenkstein aus Marmor für den hohen Offizier . . .

Monument en marbre pour le noble officier . . .

. . . en het eenvoudige houten kruis voor den „gewonen soldaat".

. . . and a simple wooden cross for the „private".

. . . und das einfache Holzkreuz für den „Gemeinen".

. . . et la pauvre croix en bois pour le 'simple soldat'.

Russisch soldatenkerkhof. (Hoe hooger het kruis is, hoe hooger de rang
van de soldaten. Onder de heel kleine kruisen liggen de gewone soldaten)

Russian soldier's cemetery. (The higher the cross, the higher the rank of
the soldiers. Under the very tiny crosses lie the „privates".)

Russischer Soldatenfriedhof. (Je höher das Kreuz, um so höher der Rang
der Soldaten. Unter den ganz kleinen Kreuzen liegen die Gemeinen.)

Cimetière militaire russe. (Plus haute la croix, plus haut le rang du soldat.
Sous les croix toutes petites les simples soldats sont couchés.)

230

Links ligt 1 officier begraven. — Rechts liggen 91 „gewone soldaten" in den grond gestopt.

To the left lies 1 officer buried. — To the right lie 91 "privates" heaped together.

Links liegt 1 Offizier bestattet. — Rechts liegen 91 „Gemeine" verscharrt.

A gauche 1 officier est enseveli. — A droite 91 'simples soldats' sont enterrés.

Soldatenkerkhof in Wilna-Antokol. (In elk graf de zoon van eene moeder.)
„Duizend kruisen staan en verkondigen
Duitschland, hoe gy trouw hebt gezaaid."
(Dominee Walter Nithak-Stahn. Paaschpreek 1915.)

Soldier's cemetery in Wilna-Antokol. (Under each grave lies a mother's son.)
„A thousand crosses stand and proclaim
Germany! how faithfully thou hast sown."
(Pastor Walter Nithak-Stahn. Easter Sermon 1915.)

Soldatenfriedhof in Wilna-Antokol. (Unter jedem Grab einer Mutter Sohn.)
„Tausend Kreuze stehen und künden,
Deutschland, wie Du treu gesät."
(Pfarrer Walter Nithak-Stahn. Osterspruch 1915.)

Cimetière militaire à Wilna-Antokol. (Sous chaque tombeau le fils d'une
mère.)
'Allemagne, des milliers de croix
Font témoignage de ta bonne semence.'
(Sentence du curé Walter Nithak-Stahn. à Pâques 1915.)

Edward Grey: „De zaak gaat zooals gewoonlyk, verder."

Edward Grey: „Business is as usual."

Edward Grey: „Das Geschäft geht wie gewöhnlich weiter."

Edward Grey: 'Les affaires prennent leur cours ordinaire.'

Die nervenschwache deutsche Polizei.

Sofort nach Erscheinen der ersten Auflage des Werkes „Krieg dem Kriege" verbot die Berliner Polizei den Arbeiter-Buchhandlungen, die Bilder aus diesem Buch im Schaufenster öffentlich auszustellen.

Da die Buchhandlung des Verlages „Freie Jugend" dagegen protestierte und die Bilder nicht freiwillig aus dem Schaufenster entfernte, kamen zwei preußische Polizisten und ein Kriminalbeamter und entfernten g e w a l t s a m , m i t d e m S e i t e n g e w e h r , diese Bilder. Ueber diese „Tat" stellte die Polizei folgende Quittung aus:

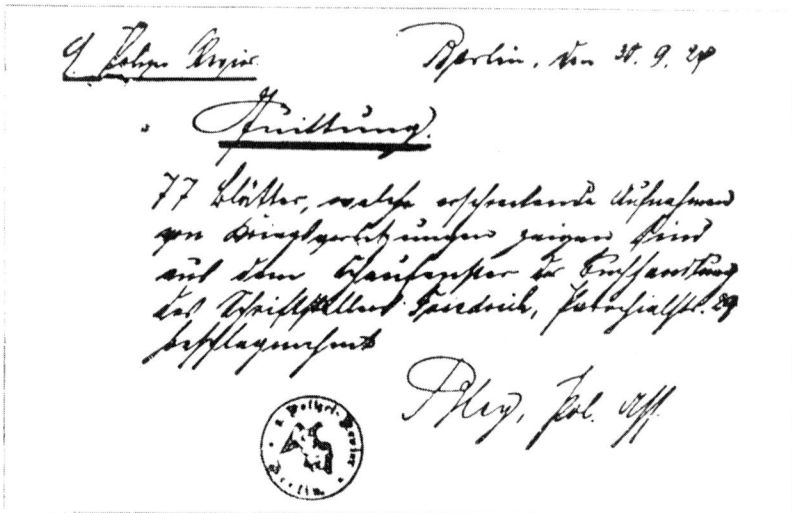

Die gesamte friedensfreundliche Presse und Oeffentlichkeit legte sofort Protest ein gegen diese Polizei-Politik, und nur diesem Umstande ist es wohl zu verdanken, daß die deutsche Republik nicht als **erste** in der Rubrik auf Seite 3 dieses Buches eingetragen ist.

La police allemande mécontente.

Aussitôt après la publication de la première édition de cette œuvre, la police berlinoise défendait à toutes les librairies d'ouvriers à Berlin d'étaler en public les images de ce livre; comme la librairie de l'éditeur de la „Freie Jugend" protesta et ne voulu pas enlever volontairement les gravures du vitrage, deux agents de police et un criminaliste arrivèrent et, avec leurs baïonnettes, ôterent ces images. Pour cette "action" la police donna le reçu ci-dessous.

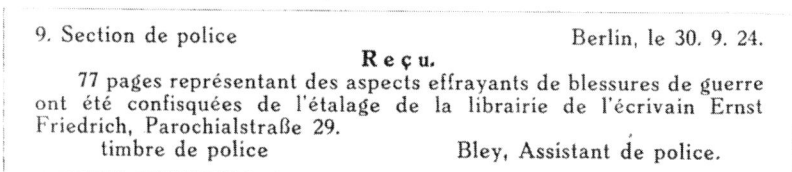

9. Section de police   Berlin, le 30. 9. 24.

R e ç u.

77 pages représentant des aspects effrayants de blessures de guerre ont été confisquées de l'étalage de la librairie de l'écrivain Ernst Friedrich, Parochialstraße 29.

timbre de police   Bley, Assistant de police.

234

Toute la presse pacifique protesta immédiatement contre cette mesure de la police, il est probablement dû à cette seule circonstance, que la république allemande ne soit pas inscrite la première dans la rubrique à la **page 3 de ce livre.**

Den nervos tyske politi.

Straks efter utgaven av det 1. oplag av vaerket "Krig mot krig" forbod berliner politiet arbeiderbokhandlerne at offentlig utstille billederne av denne bok.

Da forlaget "Freie Jugends" bokhandel protesterte derimot og ikke frivillig fjernet billederne av vinduet, kom to proissiske politibetjenter od en kriminalbetjent og fjernet disse med bajonetten. Over denne "dad" utstedte politiet folgende kvittering:

---

9. Politidistrikt.   Berlin. 30. 9. 24.
Kvittering.
77 blade, som viste skrekkelige fotografier av krigssarede, er beslaglagt av vinduet i forfatteren Friedrichs bokhandel, Parochial-straße 29.
(Politistempel)   B l e y , Politiassistent.

Hele den fredsvenlige presse og offentlighet nedla protest mot denne politi-politik og kun denne omstaendighet kan man takke for, at den tyske republik ikke er innfort som den f o r s t e i rubriken pa side 3 i denne bok.

The weak-nerved German Police.

Immediately after the appearance of the first edition of the present work, the Berlin police ordered the publishers of the journal „Freie Jugend" to remove the varous photographs, taken from the book, which had been on exhibition in their shop-window. The police further prohibited all the other workers' bookshops in Berlin from public exhibiting any pictures from this book.

As the publishers of "Freie Jugend refused to carry out the orders of the police, two officials of the Prussian Police accompanied by an official of the Secret Police entered the bookshop, u s e d t h e i r b a y o n e t s t o r e m o v e t h e p i c t u r e s that had been pasted on the window, and confiscated almost all of them.

For these "trophies" the Police gave the following receipt:—

9th Police Station.   Berlin, 30. 9. 24.
Acquittance.
77 leaflets showing terrible pictures of wounds and mutilations caused by the War, are hereby confiscated from the bookshop of the author Friedrich, Parochialstraße 29.
Stamp.   (Sd)   Bley, Police Assistant.

The entire pacifist and anti-militarist press raised a cry of protest against these police tactics, and it is due to this fact alone that the German Republic is not the first to have its name inscribed on page 3 of this book.

a) Forlaget "Freie Jugend" med en vindusutstilling av billeder av boken: "Krig mot krig."

a) The shop-window of the publishing house „Freie Jugend" with an exhibition of pictures from the book "W a r   a g a i n s t   w a r".

a) Das Schaufenster des Verlages „Freie Jugend" mit einer Ausstellung von Bildern aus dem Buch: „Krieg dem Kriege."

a) L'étalage de l'édition "Freie Jugend" avec une partie des gravures tirées du livre "Guerre à la guerre."

b) Detsamme vindu efter at berliner politiet den 30. september 1924 hadde fjernet billederne.

Man ser ennu tydelig de små papirrester av de med bajonetten nedrevne billeder.

---

b) The same shop-window a f t e r the violent removal of the pictures by the Berlin Police on the 30th of september 1924.

b) Dasselbe Schaufenster nach der gewaltsamen Entfernung der Bilder durch die Berliner Polizei am 30. September 1924.

Man sieht noch deutlich die kleinen weißen Papierfetzen, der — mit dem Bajonett — heruntergerissenen Bilder.

b) Le même étalage après l'enlévement des gravures par la police berlinoise, le 30 septembre 1924.

On voit encore distinctement les petits chiffons de papier des gravures enlevées avec la baïonnette.

Nachwort

Wenn in diesem Buch Photographien veröffentlicht sind, die vorwiegend Grausamkeiten des d e u t s c h e n Militarismus zeigen, oder besser gesagt: Grausamkeiten des Militarismus auf deutscher Seite (denn in Wahrheit ist der Militarismus ein i n t e r n a t i o n a l e s Verbrechen, ebenso wie der Kapitalismus), so will ich damit keinesfalls gesagt haben: „Seht, zu solchen Bestialitäten ist nur die deutsche Soldateska fähig." Im Gegenteil beweisen ja gerade die von französischen Truppen zerstörten F r i e d - h ö f e — wie grausam, nicht einmal den Toten den „Frieden" zu gönnen —, daß in a l l e n Soldatenröcken die Bestie steckt und daß sie kaum mehr zu bändigen ist, wenn sie erst einmal Blut geleckt hat!

Ueber vier Jahre haben a l l e kriegsteilnehmenden Nationen mit Feuer und Stahl, mit Gift und Gas Menschenmord begangen. Alle haben sich gegenseitig erschlagen, erstochen, erschossen, vergiftet, verbrannt. Wer kann aufstehen und sagen: die deutsche oder die französische, die englische oder die italienische Soldateska hat größere Brutalitäten begangen? Der Deutsche rannte mit derselben Begeisterung dem Franzosen das Bajonett in die Därme, wie der Franzose dem Deutschen den Leib aufschlitzte. Der Italiener zerschmetterte in gleichem Blutrausch dem Oesterreicher den Schädel wie umgekehrt, und der Engländer und Amerikaner torpedierten deutsche Schiffe genau so gewissenlos, wie die deutsche Marine „feindliche" Dampfer versenkte.

Wenn trotzdem v o r w i e g e n d deutsche Schandtaten hier gezeigt sind, so liegt das lediglich nur daran, daß mir, als einem zufällig in Deutschland geborenen Menschen, naturgemäß die meisten Photographien von „Deutschen" zur Verfügung standen. Um diesem Uebel abzuhelfen, ergeht daher ein

Aufruf

an a l l e Menschen a l l e r Länder

mir weiteres Bildmaterial zur Verfügung zu stellen. Ich bitte daher: Sendet mir per „Einschreiben" Kriegsphotographien, Kriegsberichte, Befehle, Aussprüche usw., damit das seit Jahren gesammelte Material recht vollständig wird und das von mir gegründete

Internationale Anti-Kriegsmuseum

immer mehr ergänzt und erweitert wird. Auch Plakate, Bilder, Lieder, Gedichte, Bücher, Soldatenspielzeug, Kriegsandenken, Nippsachen, mit Kriegssprüchen bemalte Kaffeetassen, Taschentücher, auf denen Kriegsbilder aufgedruckt sind, kurzum: alles, was mit Militarismus und Krieg i r g e n d w i e zusammenhängt oder darauf hinweist, wird für dieses

Museum dringend gesucht. Die eingesandten Photographien und Gegenstände werden auf Wunsch wieder zurückgesandt, nachdem wir für das Museum eine Kopie hergestellt haben.

Adresse:

Ernst Friedrich, Berlin C 2, Parochialstraße 29.

1. International Anti-War Museum, Berlin C 2.

---

1. Musée International contre la guerre, Berlin C 2.

Dank sage ich

dem Gesinnungsfreund R ö t t c h e r vom Verlag „Friede durch Recht" in Wiesbaden für das zur Verfügung gestellte Bildermaterial. Einige Bilder sind der leider nicht mehr erscheinenden Zeitschrift „Freie Welt" (Org. der USPD.) entnommen. Dank aber auch den vielen Gesinnungsfreunden, die mir Bilder zur Verfügung stellten. Leider kann ich aber hier nicht alle namentlich anführen. Den Uebersetzern: P. Hoffer, Zürich (franz.) und dem Genossen V. Chattopadhyaya (engl.) ebenfalls herzlichsten Dank.

Dank auch meinen Peinigern!

Endlich aber auch Dank den deutschen Staatsanwälten, die zwar einige Klischees während der Drucklegung beschlagnahmt (gestohlen) haben, die aber andererseits durch meine wiederholte kürzere und längere Inhaftierung wesentlich zur Vervollkommnung dieses Buches beigetragen haben, denn in der Abgeschlossenheit meiner Zelle kam ich auf immer neue und bessere Ideen. Diese Staatsanwälte haben mithin nicht unwesentlich — wenn auch ungewollt — unser Werk gefördert.

Born in 1894, Ernst Friedrich opened the first international anti-war museum in 1925 in Berlin. In 1930 he was nominated for the Nobel Peace Prize. In 1933 he fled the Nazis to Belgium, and again to France in 1940, where he joined the resistance. Friedrich died in 1967 in Le Perreux-sur-Marne.

The Anti-Kriegs-Museum today

The Anti-Kriegs-Museum in Berlin was reopened on 2 May 1982 – the 15th anniversary of Ernst Friedrich's death. It provides information about Friedrich's campaigning against war, with exhibits comprising both historic and contemporary material on the theme of war and peace. Its authentic World War Two air-raid shelter and the Peace Gallery help make the ideas of pacifism and international understanding accessible even for young people.

The museum is free to visit and open daily 4-8pm.

Anti-Kriegs-Museum
Brüsseler Straße 21, 13353 Berlin

Tel. 00 49 30-45490110
To arrange a group visit: 00 49 30-4028691

www.anti-kriegs-museum.de